Also by Monty Roberts
The Man Who Listens to Horses

SHY BOY
THE HORSE THAT CAME IN FROM THE WILD

MONTY ROBERTS

Photographs by Christopher Dydyk

HarperCollins*Publishers*

HarperCollinsPublishers
77-85 Fulham Palace Road
Hammersmith, London W6 8JB

Published by HarperCollins*Publishers* 1999
1 3 5 7 9 8 6 4 2

First published in Germany by
Gustav Lubbe Verlag 1998

A catalogue record for this book
is available from the British Library

ISBN 0 00 257105 6

Set in Minion

Printed and bound by The Bath Press, Glasgow

CONTENTS

ADMONITION

Working with horses has inherent dangers. Working with wild horses is generally more dangerous than working with domestic ones, and every precaution should be taken to be as safe as you possibly can should you decide to act hands on. Seek professional help, learn the language of Equus, and exercise the greatest of caution whenever you're working with horses.

ACKNOWLEDGEMENTS

Many people have assisted me in the creation of this book.

Christopher Dydyk is a talented young man with a bright future and, if he continues to produce photographs that are works of art, his talents will soon be recognized the world over.

My wife, Pat, set aside her own creative endeavour – equine sculpture – for many weeks on end and helped the book to completion, and me, in innumerable ways. I cannot thank her enough.

Many others gave encouragement. Susan Watt in London and Trena Keating in New York admirably represented HarperCollins, and demonstrated how deeply they care about the book. Louise Dennys, of Knopf Canada, continues to be the author's dream. Consistently, Louise steps up with solutions. Finally, sincere thanks to my British agent, Jane Turnbull.

PROLOGUE

As far as I am concerned, the story of Shy Boy began during a tour of the United Kingdom in 1996. Shy Boy himself wouldn't have known a thing about it at that time, of course: he was concerned only with the politics of herd life, the business of survival. He didn't know of any other place but the high desert of Nevada, the roof of the world with horizons as big as anywhere.

On the other hand, with a bit of poetic licence, you can say I've had my eye on him for forty-five years. I didn't know it would be him exactly, but it would be one of his kind. He was a vision waiting for me. But it would take an incredibly lucky set of circumstances, a whole lot of good fortune and some hard work to bring us together.

For this tour we'd put on an expanded demonstration. I had flown over Dually, my world class western competition horse, to demonstrate what he could do. Many people had asked me, 'What next?' They'd seen me start raw horses, but how did my methods work out in the long run? Dually is the answer to that question. He works with hardly a touch of the reins and his speed and agility are second to none.

Yet, despite the apparent fact that my life perhaps could be described as on a high point, there was something nagging at me. It was this. I'd left something out of my autobiography. Even after all these years, there was one particular event which I still couldn't bring myself to relate for fear of ridicule.

I'd not been entirely candid in telling my life story.

And here I was signing these piles of books until my wrist ached. To see people walking away having bought copies of my book was a rewarding experience. I'd emptied my life into that book and it contained the sum total of my experience and the reasoning behind the message I am always striving to deliver to the world: let's make the world a better place for the horse.

Except, I'd left one thing out. There had been difficult passages for me to write and experiences which were hard to bring out in the open. In particular, to reveal my father's harsh treatment of me and of the animals in his care

9

was an emotional and disturbing experience. My father's violence culminated in his beating a black man when he was an officer in the police force. This event, which I witnessed as a boy of eight, still lives with me; and on that very day I can identify my change in direction, to take the opposite way of life from my father's, to aim for kindness instead of cruelty, co-operation instead of coercion. The black man died four days later.

If I could reveal these troubling ghosts from my past life, then why couldn't I relate this one event which on the face of it would seem to be an easier tale to tell? I told this same story in 1952, only to face rejection from all fronts. I've lived with this feeling for half a lifetime, as readers of my first book will know. Yet, before this tour is finished, a set of circumstances would be set in motion which would allow me to let this story out, finally. And not only that, but to recreate the story, not just for my friends and family, but under the critical gaze of documentary cameras. I had no idea, but fate was waiting in the wings. A mustang and I were destined to come together.

ON A COLD MOONLIGHT NIGHT

It is my intention to escort you through the thirty months of my life between the publication of *The Man Who Listens to Horses* and the launch of *Shy Boy*.

The mustang became Shy Boy to me and ultimately to the rest of the world on the night of March the 30th, 1997. I was in the high desert wilderness of central California attempting to prove to the world what I had done forty-five years previously.

The moon lit our private world out there. No one else was in sight. It was two horses, one domestic and one wild, and myself.

Big Red Fox, my tall bay, settled into a routine: he watched the mustang and when the mustang moved, he moved. When the wild one stopped to graze or take water, Big Red Fox stopped, too. Foxy learned this game pretty fast and I soon realised I didn't have to direct him at all. He'd taken a position around fifty yards away from the mustang and maintained it on his own initiative.

Around ten o'clock it was getting very cold. I noticed that the comet Hale-Bopp was directly overhead, dragging its enormous tail across the night sky. It was an incredible sight in that thin air without any city lights to dilute the darkness; the comet was so clear it seemed you might reach out and pluck it from the sky. It was an awesome sight as I watched it proceed westward and then I dropped my line of sight and saw the mist.

A layer of sea fog was creeping up from the Pacific Coast around fifty miles away, steady at around my level which in the Cuyama Valley is around 3,500 feet above the sea, and it was like the sea itself rising to envelop us.

At eleven o'clock the mist layer engulfed those miles of wilderness and shut off the moon, as if it had been on a switch. I could see nothing whatsoever, which meant it was going to be nearly impossible to carry on. We'd planned to have moonlight, but could only hope against hope not to have cloud cover spoil our plans. Because my vision is only in black and white I can see better than normal sighted people in the dark, but this was useless to me. I couldn't see a thing. We were staring disaster in the face.

I was unhappy, of course, as you can imagine. I was thinking we were going to lose this mustang; we might spend the whole week searching for him. I'd look quite an idiot, coming out of the mist tomorrow morning with nothing but a sore back to show for the previous twenty-four hours.

Then, we had a further stroke of good luck. My saddle horse, Big Red Fox, stepped up to the challenge and kept me on the mustang's path. Big Red Fox would stop, start, take a right, hang a left, without instruction from me. As far as I was concerned, we could have been riding with our eyes shut. It was like the mustang was wearing a tracking device. Obviously Big Red Fox could see the mustang, smell him or sense him – I don't have the answer to this miracle – but whichever it was, he kept on him because every now and again I'd hear the click of a hoof on a stone or I'd see a faint silhouette in the mist or hear the mustang's feet as he made a quick move and I'd know we were still on track.

It raised the hairs on the back of my neck, this eerie scene. My job was to sit tight, drop the reins and try to stay warm under my many layers of clothing. It was as though we were following a ghost.

During these shadowy glimpses of the mustang, it seemed to me he was crouching, head and neck very low, using every ravine and crevice to reduce his profile and make himself harder to see. I found myself repeating the words, 'Hey, little Shy Boy, are you trying to get lost from me?'

I was shivering with cold and this repeated sentence developed a few more offshoots and turned into a song that I built up and repeated, partly to keep my energy focused, partly to take my mind off freezing, but mostly to let him know from the kindness in my voice that I meant him no harm. I can still turn back the clock and remember this little song I repeated over and over:

Hey, little Shy Boy, where are you going?
  Stop trying to hide from me
  I'll be here come morning when there's light for me to see

Hey, little Shy Boy, don't be afraid
    I'm not going to hurt you. That's a promise made.

Fifty years back, and to your kin
    My word was, it'll be better than it's been

I told them I'd leave the world a better place
    For both you horses and the human race

Hey, little Shy Boy, settle down
    Eat, drink, stop running around

You think I might hurt you, but that can't be
    Because of a promise I've made, you see

No pain to horses. Now that's my goal
    It's my life's work. I'll take this role

Shy Boy, Shy Boy, don't be so shy
    I know we'll be friends in the by and by.

ON TOUR

The events of the UK tour were memorable, even though only one part of it is the cradle of the mustang story. I want however to bring you additional episodes that were important to my experience.

First of all, this was a serious adventure and I'd like to relate the scale of the operation. To start at the beginning, I was hauling a massive amount of equipment, and two horses, from our home, Flag Is Up Farms, near Solvang, California, down to Los Angeles International Airport, called LAX for short. We'd flown horses many times before to racetracks, but this was on a different scale.

We were on our way to England and Ireland and we weren't going to the races. We were taking a very special horse on a demonstration tour. We were facing a gruelling schedule of twenty-two venues around England and Ireland, showing what this horse could do. With only a day between the demonstrations, when we weren't in the arena, we'd be travelling.

The horse's name was Dually and he's my number one friend and colleague in the show ring. His name comes from a type of pick-up truck with powerful rear axle and wheels to take extra load. Dually's certainly built with extra strength and power in his rear quarters. What he can't do in the area of western-style show events, can't be done.

He is a true example of what my training methods can achieve. To put it in a nutshell, if you can use your skills as a trainer to open a door that a horse wants to go through, then you have a horse that's your willing partner instead of your unwilling subject. With the horse's agreement and co-operation, you can create an additional momentum towards achievement which is unstoppable.

Dually and a back-up horse called Tuffy were on their way to Europe to show what they could do. And as it turned out, the first thing that looked to cause a problem was myself.

When we got to the airport, I felt this virus literally steal up from behind and try to knock me off my feet. I knew which virus it was – I'd just come back from a sale in Kentucky and my German clients had arrived at that sale carrying the virus and all had been extremely ill. It was a killer and I'd shared a motor vehicle with it for a seven or eight day period, so it had plenty of time to get its hooks into me.

I went to the hospital there at the LAX and luckily for me I stumbled on this wonderful doctor who'd come from India to work in California. I told him that it felt like the bottom half of my lungs were filled with fluid and that the pain was excruciating across my chest. He listened to my chest and agreed. He diagnosed a condition called 'walking pneumonia' with a forty per cent reduction in my breathing capacity. He ordered immediate rest.

You can imagine, I was just minutes away from having parked all of my equipment and the two horses, all of it being prepared for loading on to a KLM 747 jumbo jet. I had round trip tickets in my pocket, a schedule of demonstrations stretching ahead of us for the next three weeks, all co-ordinated with the launch of the book. This was a massive project having taken a year to put into place.

This virus was . . . well, it wasn't what I wanted to hear. I told him, 'You've told me the bad news, now it's my turn to tell you the worse news. I have to go to England, there is no option!'

He advised me, in so many words, that if I went ahead with this trip I might arrive in a wooden box and without a whole lot to say to my audience. I had to reply that whether I arrived in a wooden box or upright and walking on my own two feet, I was going all the same. I'd agree to be one hundred per cent diligent in taking any medication he suggested, but he had to know that I was on my way.

He didn't like it.

The fellow who was in charge of shipping us and who'd given me a ride to the doctor's, now gave me a ride to the pharmacy. The prescription was for Genomycin and I immediately began taking those pills with something like religious fervour.

Back at LAX, we were ready to load up and KLM was having a fit at the amount of equipment we had with us. They hollered and pointed at their lists, but couldn't fault us. I'd been over that list countless times and every article we had with us was on the list given to them. It was just that everything was bigger than they expected. For the airline executive reading the lists over in Amsterdam, 'saddles' meant racing saddles, or English saddles, not these monsters weighing fifty pounds apiece.

As a result, there wasn't a thing they could do but squeeze everything in.

It's an amazing process, being loaded into the rear end of a jumbo jet. They lift you three storeys high on these scissor lifts and then push you in with a load of televisions, electronic equipment and so one. Horses are like just another box of 'stuff' to be hauled into position and locked down. Also keeping us company were six coffins of people who had recently died in California to be returned to their families in Europe. I remembered the doctor's advice, I could be arriving in a wooden box myself.

They locked my pallet down with horses in two stalls and the third stall full to the brim with equipment. There was a four foot alley in front of the horses for the attendant to squeeze by, except in our case we had too much equipment so the access was blocked. I had to wrestle my way through and climb over our tack to check the horses and to give them food and water, to rub their faces and tell them they were thirty thousand feet about the earth with nothing holding them up except seven miles of air.

I could pass through the little door at the back of the plane marked 'Crew Only' where I had a seat reserved in the last row.

It amused me to think I was sitting next to people who had no idea Dually and Tuffy were standing a few feet behind them, just the other side of the bulkhead, on this very proper and civilised airplane with drinks handed to you by a good-looking hostess and so on. Also, what must they have thought of this guy who sounded like he was having an asthma attack and who plainly wasn't dressed as a KLM employee, ducking back through this door marked 'Crew Only.' I often wonder when I'm on a jumbo if there's a horse or two aboard. I always send them a message of sympathy. It's a cramped, nerve-racking experience for them.

In fact, it's worth taking a moment to add up what a momentous journey it was for these two horses, which puts their co-operation and their stunning performances during the tour in perspective.

The had three hours from Flag Is Up Farms to LAX. They had an eight hour layover at their airport while they had their skin scraped, their blood tested and the conditions of their thirty day quarantine checked over in minute detail. Then there was the thirteen hour flight to Amsterdam, a three hour layover in Amsterdam for the veterinarian to check them over and see to it that everything was true and accurate in the Los Angeles veterinarian's account. That's twenty-seven hours so far. We then had to load them on to an English horse van and drive them to Calais to catch a ferry for Dover. From Dover it was to Lambourn into Dougy Marks' stable, for a total of forty-seven hours.

I was able to exercise them at each transition point, but it was an incredible journey and they stood up to it with more patience and co-operation than I had the right to expect.

We were in England. There were three days before my first event and my health seemed to be improving.

As I've already mentioned, this tour was different.

Readers of my first book will be familiar with the reasons why I felt compelled to show the world what I could do with horses, but for the sake of those who haven't read the first book, I'll give a short explanation of why I do what I do and how come this tour was different. I will be as concise as possible, but this part has to be done to make sense of the whole premise of this story.

Firstly, the reader should understand that I was born on a horse. I was up there on the saddle in front of my mother for hours at a time from the day I could hold my head up. I was more familiar with the sight of a horse's neck and the way their ears talk back and forth, then any other sight. I won my first trophy at the age of four.

My family ran a horse facility in California dealing with hundreds of horses on a daily basis. I was mucking out twenty-two stalls a day before school from the age of eleven.

My early success in the show ring led my father to believe I was going to be the one to make the name of Roberts famous in the world of horses.

Yet, I had this dilemma. I watched my father 'breaking in' horses and I was repelled by the violence involved in the traditional methods he used. I watched him tie up six horses at a time in a corral, the horses evenly spaced, each one at its post. He proceeded to tie up their hind legs so they were incapable of moving and then he'd deliberately frighten them by throwing a weighted sack at their hindquarters. Of course, they showed resistance and fear at this approach, whereupon his response was to coerce them into submission. It was his view that when they were totally submissive and showed no defiance no matter what you did to rile them, then he'd broken them. It took four to six weeks.

And 'broken' was the right word. You had horses who were traumatised, working only out of fear. You had horses who never forgave the pain they'd suffered, who never joined up with a human being, out of emotional need or affection or any other laudable motive. You had tyranny.

I was watching this from an early age, and I found it repulsive.

Yet this man was my father. He was admired and respected. This way of dealing with horses was the norm, and still is in many places in the world, more places than you'd think.

What turned me against my father as much as his cruelty to animals was his cruelty to me. He beat me with chains and I ended up in the hospital with my mother begging me to pretend it was an accident; she'd have a word with my father and change his behaviour. I learned to fear him and his desire to subordinate and humiliate those near to him, whether animal or human.

As the same time, I learned I had an affinity with horses. I could watch them forever. Just by being passive, by allowing them their natural behaviour I began to piece together the way they communicated with each other.

Between the ages of thirteen and seventeen, I had the opportunity of passing extended time on the high ranges of Nevada, completely alone and watching herds of mustangs so wild they'd perhaps never set eyes on a human being.

*Previous page: A misty morning with
Monty and Dually.*

*Above: Strategy session, Pat and Monty
with a BBC QED film maker.*

Above: Freddy at the Maverick Saloon.

Overleaf: 'The ranch herd.'

Previous page: Herding horses on the
high desert.

Above: Monty on Dually and Cathie
Twissleman on a ranch horse. Shy Boy is
the third horse from the left. 'Beginning
to cut him out'.

Above: Monty on Dually and Cathie Twissleman on a ranch horse, with Shy Boy just in front of them. 'Taking flight'.

Overleaf: Monty on Dually. Shy Boy now singled out.

Monty enjoying the challenge.

Above: Shy Boy trying to get back to the herd. Dually doing his job.

Overleaf: Cathie assisting Monty as Shy Boy tests them.

I had this opportunity because I was part of a group charged by the town of Salinas, California, to round up a group of these mustangs for the annual rodeo event, the wild horse race. In travelling to the high desert of Nevada and observing these wild herds, my first realisation was that the matriarch of the herd was in charge. She was the social leader. She was the one who chose when to move and where to go.

Most significantly, she was the one who kept the youngsters in order. The adolescents, if they misbehaved, had her to deal with. She had a particular way of doing it, and no doubt this method is engraved in the genetic, tribal memory of the horse around the world. Because, as I have proved, it always works.

If one of those adolescents misbehaves, if he or she takes a bite out of an elder's rump or kicks out or is high-handed, in short, if he or she is anti-social, then the matriarch drives the offender out of the herd. She squares up to the delinquent, drives him out and stays squared up to him until she sees the signs that show her he's asking forgiveness, he's asking to be let back in.

The offender, of course, is frightened. It's no place for a horse to be, outside the herd. There are predators out there. To be away from the herd is to sign your own death warrant. The elders of the herd, who'd outlived their usefulness, would often take themselves off, deliberately walk into a place of solitude, asking to die.

When the predicament of the adolescents sink in, that they were evicted from the herd, then these offenders would ask to be let back into the group. They'd offer recognisable signals, asking forgiveness. They'd lick and chew, the mouthing action of the dependent asking for food from a superior, showing submission. They'd drop their noses close to the ground, again a gesture of submission.

At this point the matriarch would respond. She'd turn, change her attitude. She'd neglect to maintain eye contact. She'd show her flank, rather than

Opposite: Separate now, Monty and Shy Boy begin the journey.

adopt the square-on position as previously. These were the signs from her that the offender had been forgiven. The offender saw them, and knew that permission had been granted him to join the herd again.

I became very excited at this stage of my life, recognising this body language. I gave the language a name, Equus. I learned it and how to use it. I found that I could communicate with horses, however wild they were.

I discovered at an early age that, by using this language of Equus, I could have a wild horse following me around like I was the matriarch. It was extraordinary, but it was a process I could and did, prove again and again. It was measurable, it could be repeated. It was predictable. It held up to the most scientific analysis of animal behaviour. It was a language that I proved could be communicated inter species. I learned to listen to horses.

For a full account of that process, and those extraordinary trips to the high desert of Nevada, I'd refer you to my first book. Suffice it to say that my discovery of Equus in my teenage years led directly to the types of demonstrations I felt driven to perform in front of audiences around the world, albeit over forty years later.

I didn't do so earlier simply because my concepts were not accepted. I learned not to say a word. If I mentioned it, I was punished severely. Instead I went about practising my methods in secret, until I was old enough to leave home and start my own horse operation. Even then, I kept quiet. It was something that brought me nothing but trouble, but at the same time I knew, deep in my heart, it was the way.

All this is to explain that when recognition came to me, relatively late in life, I seized it with both hands. I wanted this out in the open. I'd believed in it and had it locked up in me for so long, that now it's out and recognised, I'm like a demon with it. I want everyone to know. I'll go to the ends of the earth to show what I can do.

I can take an untrained horse and normally within seven to ten minutes I will have him 'joined-up' with me; that's to say, he will follow me wherever I go in the round pen, his nose to my shoulder. Within twenty minutes, he will be standing quietly, without any manner of restraint attached to his head, while I ask him to accept the saddle, and then the bit and bridle. Within half an hour, there will be someone riding that horse. There won't have been a cruel word, not a sign of a whip or a spur or any kind of restraint.

This process, which I call 'starting' rather than 'breaking' would have taken my father up to six weeks and would have involved inflicting much pain. With my way of 'join-up', it normally takes less than thirty minutes and no pain whatsoever.

And I have demonstrated this method of starting horses thousands of times, literally, in front of many thousands of people, all over the world.

During a typical event I start maybe two raw horses and, while I do so, I explain to the audience what to look out for. I predict when it's going to happen and describe what I will do next. However, this particular tone was a special occasion as I've said and I wanted to do something extra for this to coinside with the launch of the book. I had to ask myself, what questions were people asking the most? What would answer that question so it would be the most interesting thing I could provide for them?

A question I've often been asked during my demonstrations is, what next? How do your methods work out? It's all very well giving your horse this benevolent start in life, but how does that translate, later on, in the adult horse?

I decided to bring over Dually and show everyone. This was a horse trained using my methods. These methods had taken him right up to world class status.

Of course, this would be more interesting to an English audience than to an American one because Dually is a cutting horse, and for an English person to see reining and cutting is unusual in itself, let alone to see it done to the impressive standard set by Dually, a triple crown champion in the United States.

We expanded the round pen and, in addition to booking raw horses for the demonstrations, we booked cattle.

Dually would work these cattle without even a bridle. He's such an intelligent and willing horse, he's able to cut a cow from a herd and hold it at bay, separate from the herd, whatever twists and turns the cow might try. He'll do this of his own accord, without a sign from me. He knows exactly what to do and wants to do it for himself. It's as much as I can do to hang on. I have enlisted Dually as a willing participant in the event that I myself wish him to perform and the result is pretty amazing.

Meanwhile, Tuffy would be on turn-back duty, rolling the cows back in the far end of the pen to increase the challenge to Dually. Tuffy would act as the back-up horse as well. As it turned out, it was as well we had the back-up capability, as a farrier inadvertently put a nail through the wrong spot in Dually's hind shoe in Ireland and Tuffy had to play the lead for a couple of nights.

On a technical note, there was a couple of interesting points about this particular tour.

Firstly, water.

It was difficult to keep Dually and Tuffy drinking. They didn't like the chlorination in the water. Whichever area of the country we visited, the water tasted of this chlorine disinfectant. When we arrived at Gleneagles, they drank and drank like crazy because the water was fresh and they probably took on four times the amount than at any other place.

With hindsight, we should have put them on a water flavouring programme before we left California. If we'd put them on an apple-flavoured electrolyte for a number of weeks back home, when we got over there, we could have used the same electrolyte and the familiar flavour would have masked the chlorination.

I'm quite used to doing this for sensitive race horses when they travel, but I didn't think I would have to do it for these resilient quarter horses. Yet, on occasions we had to make trips out of town to fetch untreated water from a farm to get them to drink enough.

Secondly, feed.

American hay is different from British hay. We arranged for Dually and Tuffy to have Washington state hay purchased from Barry Hills in Lambourn. He imports it for feeding to race horses, but luckily his supplier agreed to provide enough for the trip. An added advantage to this tour was to have the sponsorship of Highlight Feeds. They provided all the concentrates and the horses did extremely well on it. Highlight Feeds went to enormous trouble to help us, even when the horses' bowels tightened a little from lack of water, they brought along a little feed with bran which put matters right.

The first task was to pull all the vehicles together. We had trucks for transporting the books, the videos and other necessary equipment. Then we had the two horses and their truck. We had the cattle in their transporter, and a motor home for us.

It was a convoy.

Our first stop was Towerlands in Essex and there were several memorable responses from members of the audience.

There was a body-builder, a massively built man who worked as a London policeman. He told me that his father beat him as a child, and of course this was why he'd built himself up to such physical strength. He needed to feel he could handle anyone who physically confronted him. Not that he'd achieved his aim, he was beginning to realise that the valuable thing was to eliminate the violence from his life, not look for it.

Also, there was a woman who came up to me, to say that she was escorting to this demonstration my biggest fan whereupon she reached down and lifted a child on to her hip. 'This is Samantha,' she said, and they showed me a photograph of Samantha's horse, Bess.

'She might be a fan,' I replied, 'but she's not a very big fan.' I thought she was maybe eight or nine years of age.

'She's read your book three times,' confirmed her mother, 'so we're getting the video for her as well.'

I was impressed by the little girl's bright, intelligent expression and her serious attitude. She promised she was going to learn everything she could about horses. She said she'd be in touch with me to let me know how it was going. She asked if she might give me a hug and have her picture taken.

This direct emotional response touched me and I knew I'd always remember this little girl, whether or not we ever saw one another again. However, I was

39

destined to see Samantha again nine months later on a subsequent UK tour and it was memorable.

After that first demonstration at Towerlands we were set to visit approximately twenty-two different places in England and Ireland. Dually and Tuffy settled down and the format of the demonstration also fell into place. We'd start one green horse to demonstrate join-up, which is the central thesis of my work in communicating with horses. Then we'd have an intermission during which I'd speak to people in person and sign more books.

Meanwhile the shape of the round pen was altered to make it a larger, oval shape and I would introduce Dually. I'd put him through his paces, the lightning-fast pirouettes, the emergency stop and so on, all performed without a touch on his mouth or without picking up the reins. The emergency stop routine has him gallop full out and from there slide to a stop instantly. The only instructions he receives from me is a tightening of my seat, a slight movement of my legs and a barely perceptible lifting of the reins.

At this point, we'd bring the truck in and let the cattle into the enlarged round pen. I think people were amazed at Dually's strength and speed at cutting a cow out of the herd, keeping his eye on it, dancing back and forth, keeping his body low to the ground with his quarters tucked in under him as he pivoted from left to right. The crowd always cheered us on.

Hopefully, on this tour, people were getting a little extra. They could see how I started a young horse, but in the second part of the demonstration they could also see the level of co-operation I enjoy with Dually who truly is my partner in the western show events. He's a champion many times over and deservedly so.

To see him in action was to answer the question, 'How does your work in starting young horses translate into the adult horse?' People can see for themselves the physical and mental strength of Dually, his partnership with the rider.

Perhaps the other question I'm asked most frequently is, 'Can anyone do what you do?' and more 'Could I do what you do?' In short, people always want to know if they can follow my methods and achieve join-up by themselves.

My answer is always, 'Absolutely.' Anyone can do it. I might have been the first to happen on it, but if a person is determined and she has the confidence and sufficient ability to recognise what to do and when, then he or she can achieve join-up. I have shown many competent horse people my methods and had them up and running in no time.

I want to make it clear that one should be relatively sound physically and able to see before they attempt this technique. It is not something you can do from a wheelchair or crutches and you need to be able to see the animal in order to execute the language. I am also convinced that people who are phobically frightened of horses should not be expected to perform these tasks.

The more competent the student is at handling themselves around horses, the better their chances for success. I recommend instructions from a professional and above all utilise safe practices when handling a horse by these methods or any other.

SAMANTHA

Although I hadn't planned on it, circumstances now presented me with a very special lady who would show people it's true, most anyone can achieve join-up.

Because Samantha did get in touch with me, as she'd promised she would, a note arrived, accompanying a video tape. The tape was 'home-made' and not easy to view, but I could see Samantha in a building with a horse which quite plainly was responding to her and as I rewound the tape and looked at it several times, it became clear to me that Samantha had achieved join-up with her horse, Bess.

At the time I watched the video, I was on my next UK tour and only eight days away from the biggest demonstration of all on that tour, set for the London Docklands Arena, which has a capacity of around 5,000 people. It was also the venue closest to where Samantha lived.

I called Samantha and invited her to attend this demonstration in London, and if she could possibly summon up the courage, I'd want her to tell the audience what she'd accomplished. I also invited her to bring Bess, her horse, to show everyone.

To appreciate fully her strength of character and her motivation, it's necessary to go back in time and reveal Samantha's history.

The London Docklands Arena demonstration in the autumn of 1997 had a life of its own. I had been wanting for some time to take on one of these large arenas, have a comfortable seating arrangement and a big event for a lot of people, but only if I could do a really good job of it. It turned out to be a good decision because about 5,000 came to the Docklands Arena and we received numerous fantastic letters afterwards from attendees.

Everyone who came to the Docklands Arena will remember Samantha, a little girl rescued from the jaws of death and a pony rescued from an untimely end in the slaughter house. Everything she did, she learned by watching my video after reading the book, *The Man Who Listens to Horses*, the year before. This in itself is a remarkable achievement, but her story is even more inspiring.

Above: The aeromotor, Cuyama Valley,
Caliente Mountain.

Overleaf: Shy Boy heads east for higher
country.

43

*Previous page: On the fly, Shy Boy
headed east. Monty and Cathie staying
within eyesight.*

*Above: Shy Boy continues east. Monty
stays with him.*

Above: Headed east.

50   *Above: North-east and bending.*

Above: Headed north-east.

*Overleaf: Monty on The Cadet,
settling into a routine at sundown,
Easter Sunday.*

Overleaf (right): Shy Boy.

*Above: Join-up achieved and now
he follows.*

*Right: Monday midday, on George,
preparing to put the rope on.*

*Overleaf: 'I don't want you to put the
rope on. Please go away,' says Shy Boy.*

Above: Caleb gives assistance. Monty wants to put the rope on. Shy Boy is saying, 'I don't fear you now.'

I must backtrack here to when Samantha was about three months old. She suffered from a bad case of 'flu and from that time on developed an intolerance for almost anything and spent most of her life in hospital. Her illness was very severe. She would have fits, be in incredible pain and suffer respiratory arrest. By the time she was five years old, she weighed about twenty-eight pounds. Her parents spent most of their time taking her to and from hospitals. Great Ormond Street Children's Hospital in London became a second home for her. She lived on the edge, often her parents wondering if this would be the last time they would see her.

Eventually someone recommended that they contact Dr Jean Munroe, an allergy specialist, out in Hertfordshire. Samantha's mother was certain they were all on the wrong track and that it wasn't allergies. But, as a last ditch attempt to save her life, they took Samantha there.

This little girl aged five years was put through a programme of withdrawal from certain foods that made a 'cold turkey' programme for a heroin addict seem tame. By the third week she was much better and soon after was allowed home. At last the parents had their daughter back.

However, once during a serious crisis whilst suffering a partial arrest, Samantha's mother in desperation asked her when she got better if there was something she really wanted. 'A horse.' was her answer.

Her mother was horrified. They had never had horses and she knew absolutely nothing about them. But a promise is a promise. Once she reached twelve years old and was off the rigorous diet, antigens and pills, Samantha's mother set out to look for a horse.

As we all know, that is not an easy task, even for an expert. Anyone who has ever bought a horse has a story to tell about their experiences. This one had quite a twist to it. Her mother read about a part-bred pony for sale and made an appointment to see it. When she arrived, they led the pony around and it seemed nice, quiet and easy to manage. She was impressed. She made two more appointments to view the pony. Each time the vendors insisted on an appointment being made and the last time she went, they had the pony tacked up. Everything seemed to be ideal. She now took Samantha to see the pony, by appointment, of course, and Samantha was overjoyed.

When the pony arrived, there was quite a to-do trying to unload her. She reared, pawed and threw herself to the floor in an attempt to rid herself of the handlers. The parents were assured that it would take a few days to settle in.

Settle in, no way. Apparently this pony had no intention of co-operating with anyone. It would rear, kick out and was completely unridable. They knew then that it must have been drugged when they went to see it. The pony was so vicious that it bit the top of Samantha's fingers off and she had to have them stitched back on.

The parents finally called in professional help and sent the horse off to be schooled. It managed to fling off even an experienced horsewoman. However, after a period of time, the pony returned to Samantha a bit more tractable but still unridable. It was at this time that Samantha saw the first BBC QED documentary on television showing my 'Join-Up' methods.

Samantha started badgering her mother about this Monty Roberts chap and her mother thought I was some teenybopper pop star. Finally after some investigation, she realised that I was a horseman/author and went out to purchase the book I had written.

Samantha studied my methods all on her own without any help. She eventually gained enough confidence to attempt 'Join-Up' with her pony and to her delight and amazement, it worked. Her pony turned out to be a Russian Arabian with papers and had the name Raichia. The vendors had tricked them horribly, but they won in the end. As Samantha outgrew Raichia, she managed to sell her as a first-rate, quiet, lovable pony who had developed into a reliable mount.

Samantha brought her next horse Bess to London Docklands where she demonstrated 'Join-Up' for the audience. This horse, too, had been difficult when first purchased. However she did have a lovely temperament, consequently they wanted to persevere with her. At first when you put a saddle on her, she bucked, carried on and bolted. They found out eventually it had been caused by being tied down and climbed all over. You couldn't get near her with a whip. The parents again sent their horse to a professional trainer and it was there that they found out that she had been abused. She wasn't as severe a case as Raichia and, using 'Join-Up', Samantha has her going beautifully in show jumping and is winning awards.

Meeting Samantha at Docklands and watching this little slip of a girl in that pen was one of the most moving experiences I have had. To find this young girl had benefited from my experience and taken the language of Equus and used it successfully, was gratifying to say the least.

Samantha was the start of that show and deservedly so. She overshadowed me and everyone else. There wasn't a heart that wasn't moved, to hear her story and you could feel the flow of admiration for her, that despite her early difficulties – or perhaps because of them – she'd developed such strong character and successful attitude. Samantha made me feel I had made great strides in my overall aim, to make the world a better place for the horse. Even if there's only a few other Samanthas out there, then I've done my job and accomplished my goal.

OPPORTUNITY OF A LIFETIME

As I've mentioned before, there was one episode in my life which I left out of the last book I wrote. This was an episode which was extremely important to me and to my work, but one that I could not verify under the circumstances.

However, this one thing rankled me. I didn't like having left it out. It was part of my education. And in a way, it was among the most wonderful experiences of my teenage years.

Now, with the amount of acceptance my ideas were gaining around the world, I wanted this story told. The way in which circumstances transpired to offer me the opportunity of not only telling this story, but reliving it, is truly amazing to me at this time in my life. This is the start of a new wild horse adventure.

As I happened to be in London on tour, I was contacted by executives of BBC's QED television company, who had made the original documentary investigating the process of join-up. It had enjoyed considerable success and as a matter of course we were in discussions as to any other television programmes which might be possible.

They inquired, what's next? Is there another programme to be made with Monty Roberts? Did I have any new ideas?

I hesitated. This wasn't a small idea. In fact, it was downright monumental. There seemed no way, especially so far from England, they were going to go for it. None the less, I plunged on. I said, 'There is one story I've always wanted to relive.'

They waited patiently.

I continued, 'When I was seventeen I did actually achieve join-up with a mustang in the wild.'

There was silence. I was waiting for their disbelief. I was ready to be told this was impossible. Even to me, who'd done it all those years ago in the early 1950s, it seemed unlikely, sitting in this glass and concrete office building that anyone would go for this idea.

'What I'd like,' I went on, 'is to recreate that event, to take the principles of join-up, do it in the wild with no round pen and with a totally wild mustang. I've done it once before and I think I can do it again.'

They asked, 'What makes you think it'll happen the way you want it to?'

I explained that the principles of join-up were given me by wild horses living in natural, untouched conditions on the high desert in Nevada. It worked everywhere else in the world in a round pen with 5,000 or more people watching me, it will work in the very location where I learned it, in fact where I had already accomplished it at age seventeen.

They were interested, but quite naturally couldn't commit at the moment to the idea. It was a world away from their own. There was a lot of risk from their point of view, enormous expense of travel, film crew, director and equipment to list a few of the obstacles. The weather, snakebite, injury or failure on my part and they'd come back having spent a boat load of money with nothing to show for it. For them it was in the nature of an experiment and the financial risk would be all theirs.

I left that giant white building feeling fairly sure they'd reject the idea. Most people's assessment of the situation would have to be that a raw mustang wouldn't accept its first saddle, bridle and rider out in the wild without restraint and they weren't likely to invest enormous sums to film it.

I recall looking back at that building and thinking what a difference it could make in my life if by some miraculous turn of events they would agree to document my story.

'MESTENGO'

First, perhaps I should say a word or two about mustangs as a breed. Shy Boy is one of them and he clearly exhibits the traits of his genetic inheritance.

Shy Boy's ancestors were brought to America by the Spanish settlers who came, a few at a time at first, and then in droves in the nineteenth century. There were no indigenous horses – it's believed horses were extinct on the north American continent long before European settlers arrived – and so the wild herds could only grow from those horses which had escaped or been abandoned by the Spanish cavalry or 'conquistadors', the Spanish invaders who became the first settlers.

These were the forebears of the mustangs and they colonised the wild heartland of western United Stages. Exactly how and when the horse re-inhabited the great plains and the high desert of America is debatable. Free-ranging horses are recorded as early as 1841 in the Great Basin area. Horse tracks were found along the edge of Pyramid Lake, recorded by Fremont in his diary of 1843. Certainly, Indians knew enough to steal the horse belonging to Kit Carson, who was a member of Fremont's expedition. By 1909, there were reports of thousands of feral horses, recorded in Steel's account of trapping wild horses in Nevada.

America in the early years was a battlefield principally between the English, the Spanish and the native American Indian , and the Indian learned to ride from the Spanish settler. Therefore, the mustang has European and north African ancestry. They still show Spanish characteristics today such as their unique gait at a trot or canter.

They were tough animals; they had to be to survive the eight-week journey over to the Americas from Spain. The horses usually lived up on the main deck of the boat in appalling conditions and suffered many maladies, some fatal. It was the nature of travel in those days. It wasn't for the faint-hearted, either animal or human. The 'horse latitudes' aren't called that for a nice reason. Many horses perished there. It was the difficulties of transporting livestock across the ocean that led the Spanish to establish horse-breeding farms on Cuba.

Cortez was recorded as saying he depended on the horse for victory. Sadly, his men weren't always so reliable. Man and horse trekked across some of the most inhospitable country. They climbed mountains, forded rivers and swamps, battled through impenetrable undergrowth and, if that wasn't enough, they had the Indians to contend with. If the men were made of iron, the horses were forged of titanium.

The Spanish had centuries of horsemanship behind them. The Moors, who conquered Spain, were great horsemen and brought their unique talents with them. The Spanish brought their riding style to America and the cowboys adapted it, bringing the leg position further forward and changing the cut of the saddle. They neck-reined and held the reins above the pommel, leaving the other hand free to work the rope. To give them this free hand, they had to develop a control system that was quick, accurate and one-handed.

Ranch owners in California employed Spanish horsemen who were called 'reinsman'. They trained horses to work cattle and these reinsman could get a horse to do extraordinary things. They stopped in an instant from a full gallop, they could turn a steer as it was running along a fence or cut an individual out from the herd and hold it out, bringing it under control. The bits they used were heavier and more complicated than the simple snaffle, but the reinsman trained their horses to respond to the slightest pressure of the rein or leg, achieving an immediate, dynamic response from the slightest of signals.

Bernal Diaz, who accompanied Cortez, recorded the colours of their horses: dark and light chestnuts, light bays, dappled, almost black, piebald, golden bay, perfect bay, mahogany bay, brown and black. And these were the same colours that I would have seen on the occasion of the early trips to the high desert of Nevada, when I was between the ages of thirteen and seventeen. Except, of course, I couldn't see because of the fact that I can only see in black and white.

The word mustang is derived from the Spanish word 'mestengo' (stray beast). These early stray animals quickly reverted to a wild stage. It is quite amazing how quickly horses can go back to their purest, natural instincts and become as wild as they were thousands of years ago. Whilst there are other domestic species that possess this ability, few can match the horse.

It is recorded that these early, scanty numbers quickly multiplied and, in less than one hundred years, it is said that the count was around two million.

More than one million horses were captured by the government for use in World War I and from that point forward hundreds of thousands were shot for use in animal feeds and even for the sport of it.

In 1971, the United States congress voted in a law to protect wild horses and burros. The US government set about to appoint agencies charged with the duty to maintain appropriate numbers of mustangs on federal lands. This responsibility eventually was assigned to the Federal Bureau of Land Management (BLM). Eighty million acres in sixteen states were placed under strict management so as to protect these wild animals. During the process of creating this law it was recorded that more letters poured into congress over the plight of wild horses than any other issue in US history. One congressman is said to have received 14,000 letters. The law passed without a single dissenting vote.

It shouldn't be surprising that people feel the way they do about horses. I believe there is no other animal in human history that has had more impact on our lives than the horse. Millions gave their lives to our wars. They delivered our mail, ploughed out fields, cleared out lands and even entertained us with their athleticism.

It is currently estimated that there are something close to 30,000 free-roaming mustangs in the western United States.

Since my first contact with the American mustang in the late 1940s, I have worked with hundreds of them both in open country and in enclosures. I have as much respect for the mustang as any other breed with which I have worked around the world. Having said that, it should be noted that I have

Above: Caleb continues to assist.

*Overleaf: Getting closer now with
the rope.*

Previous page: Shy Boy's first lead rope.

Right: Monty says 'Let's go for a walk.' Shy Boy says, 'No way!'

Overleaf: Monty says, 'I beg your pardon.' Shy Boy says, 'I'll show you, Big Boy.'

72

Using join-up to request rather than demand.

Shy Boy's first girth.

Cathie and Caleb prepare the camp
for a well-deserved rest.

*Above: Monty is coming now,
all is ready.*

*Overleaf: Celeb settles in to
await Monty's arrival.*   79

Time for everybody to get some rest.

worked intensely with thoroughbreds, quarter horses, Arabians, warm bloods, most of the pony breeds and several of the draft breeds as well.

The American mustang has certainly become a diversified genetic entity. They are a tough, highly intelligent horse with physical attributes often superior to most of our domestic breeds. I believe that the American mustang should be preserved as a national treasure. Their numbers should be watched over to allow them to live along with other species, utilising the range lands where they currently exist. I find no better way to see to their best interest than through the utilisation of the BLM as an administrative agency in charge of the protection of America's wild mustang herds.

I do not feel that the BLM has always been right in every decision it has made. Nor has it been totally wrong in its decisions either. Those of us outside of the BLM have created many small groups with ideas and agendas that, while well meaning, have served to add to the problems rather than to lessen them. I am a realist and I hope that I will always utilise common sense when assessing the needs of the mustang.

There are those would kill all of the mustangs, while there are those who would encourage them to roam free without controlling their numbers. It seems to me that the best interest of the mustang lies somewhere between these two positions. I support the BLM's current adoption programme, but feel that it is in need of significant revision.

I believe that the mustang is a highly trainable animal that can serve many purposes in today's horse industry. There is no question that they can be trained to become trustworthy partners for people, providing years of service, entertainment and companionship. However, I am just as strong in my belief that, if poorly treated, they can become dangerous and destructive. Whilst mustangs should never be taken for granted by ill-prepared people who do not understand the level of competence necessary for dealing with any wild animal, it is my belief that equus in general is an often misunderstood specie and is sadly treated by many human beings in an unfair manner. When you add the aspect of non-domestic use of horses to this scenario, the level of misunderstanding seems to increase significantly.

Mustangs, raised outside the confines of domesticity, are imprinted by nature with a need to sharpen their wits and hone their cerebral processes to a degree seldom seen in the domestic horse. It should be noted that 'survival of the fittest' is responsible for weeding out a high percentage of the herds' slow thinkers at an early age. The bright, young survivors are further educated by a sociological order within the family group that constitutes an equine university.

The mustang must deal with the realities of life in the wild, which includes being attacked by cougars, coyotes or suffering as the recipient of stray or well-aimed gunfire, with the lead remaining buried in some muscle as a lifetime reminder. The mustang's experience of growing up in this harsh and sometimes unforgiving world ensures that he will either learn quickly or perish.

Mustangs miss nothing. They will notice the slightest movement within a quarter of a mile, changes in their surroundings so subtle that the domestic horse would pass them by without a notice. Their keen wits and attention to detail can be an incredible attribute or a dangerous characteristic, depending on your level of competency.

Recently I was on a mountain top in central California with four horses and three other men. We were sitting waiting for the ranch owner to arrive, when one of the horses lifted his head, shifted his legs and stood with his attention directed at something off in the distance. It just so happens that this horse was a well-trained mustang, working cattle on the ranch. He stood frozen whilst the other horses rested a hind leg, drooped their lower lips and relaxed their ears until they pointed sideways. The other three men didn't seem to notice anything, but I worked on trying to focus on the spot he seemed to be pointing out. After three or four minutes, I spotted three cows that had appeared from a draw on a hillside at least a mile away. It seemed to me that we could have spent the rest of the day there without the non-mustangs noticing them. Mustang intelligence, when properly nurtured, can be a phenomenal ally if their human companion will only take notice of the acuity of their language.

The wild horse by its very nature has developed a strength of physiological make-up that tends to help them overcome illness or injury to a degree superior to the domestic horse. Most of them are as tough as nails and had to be in order to survive on the range.

The endurance capabilities of the American mustang are legendary. Not only can they go all day for you, but they can go day after day as well. In addition, not only will they go the extra mile, but they will do it with a generosity seldom seen in the domestic horse.

One cannot list the attributes of the American mustang without making special note of their feet. While environmental factors are largely responsible for a thick hoof wall and an extremely tough sole structure, the genetics of the American mustang most often carry the influence of the north African breeds who possess hoof conformation of the highest calibre.

Sure, they're wild, and can be dangerous, but that should not suggest that one dismiss the fact that they are a wonderful, intelligent and trainable horse. Mustangs can be willing to work as partners with us, if we will but learn to understand them, trust them and treat them with respect when we bring them in from the wild.

JOIN-UP IN THE WILD

It was in 1948 that I made my first trip to Nevada. I was there, even at that young age, as part of a group who were charged to gather a certain number of mustangs to be used for the wild horse race in the town of Salinas. Readers of my first book will understand how I came to be in such a position, but suffice it to say that even by the standards of those times I was pretty young to be heading off to the high desert.

I was already fully aware of the principle of 'advance and retreat'. The theory went like this: if you push a herd of wild horses in a certain direction for a certain distance, and then lay off them, turn back, it's their natural inclination to turn themselves and follow. The Indians used this trick to capture wild herds. They'd drive the herd away for at least a day and in their wake construct a keyhole shaped structure around a quarter of a mile long, using wires, poles and brush. Then they stopped driving the herd away; the herd would bend back and follow them. A couple of riders would be spared to circle around behind the mustangs and the trap would be complete. It was not difficult to drive them into the trap which stood in their path. That was advance and retreat.

On my trips to Nevada, I spent long hours observing the wild herds. I sometimes forgot the reason I was meant to be there and was completely caught up in observing this natural phenomenon. The matriarch's (the dominant mare is the leader of the herd, not a stallion as thought by many) way of dealing with anti-social behaviour was parallel to the idea of advance and retreat. She drove the offender away and when she released the pressure on him and turned away, the offender was allowed to come back.

My desire to understand and communicate with horses was buried deep inside me and at this age was driven more by intuition than intent. It's almost as if part of me was just as much a horse as a human, I felt so drawn to watching them and attempting to make sense of their physical language.

What struck me again and again was how careful the matriarch was in her disciplining of the young, only to reward a positive action, never a negative one. At the slightest sign of the offender's returning to his old ways, he'd be driven straight back out.

In my mind, the principle of advance and retreat was linked to the way in which the matriarch disciplined the adolescent in the wild herd.

It was only a short step to realise that if it could be done with a herd of horses, then it could be done with just one, with spectacular results possible. This could be a new way of working with horses to gain their co-operation. I was convinced that it would be possible to cause a mustang to turn and come back to me of his own volition.

I went on to perform this same experiment in the round pen, back in Salinas with the mustangs we'd eventually captured for the wild horse race.

But the truth is, these theories were tested first on the high desert of Nevada, without a fence or another human being in sight.

My knowledge was limited. I was only a kid. None the less, I did spend time with one particular mustang and caused him to stop going away from me and instead to come back. I had this little mustang following me around after twenty-four hours. It was amazing. These were the wildest, untamed horses of America and here was one of them, joined up with me, inviting me to be its friend, in effect.

I thought this was an outstanding achievement and stopped short to race back to the ranch and tell people what I'd done. This was breaking new ground. It would revolutionise how we dealt with horses. I was certain the more experienced horsemen would embrace my observations and go all out to try it for themselves. I was naive.

This was plainly a wild tale by a young man with an overactive imagination. It was laughed off.

When I returned home to Salinas with the captured mustangs for the wild horse race, my father, my brother, Ray Hackworth, Tony Vargas and Dick Gillott found my tale amusing. They slapped their legs at the mention of the idea.

The following year in 1951, when I was again allowed to assist in the expedition to gather mustangs for the annual Salinas rodeo, I returned to the high desert with the aim of doing all that I could do to consolidate my experience of the previous year.

This time, I chose a male, around three or four years old, agile, fit and intelligent. Within twenty-four hours I'd reached a point where I could ask him to come back to me. With the use of my body aligned with my horse's body, I could stop him and have him follow me. This time I could get close enough to stroke him, and that was some moment, let me tell you. I leaned over and touched this wild animal who'd decided that I was all right, that I was on the same wavelength and wasn't a threat. It was as though I was one of his family members, scratching the top of his neck. It was a magical feeling. I slipped a loose rope around his neck and schooled him to lead alongside my saddle. He wasn't particularly resentful of that because join-up had already been successful. As far as he was concerned, we were both on the same team.

I took a surcingle and placed it over his back. Not wanting to risk going under his belly to catch the other end, I fashioned a piece of wire into a long hook and used it to bring the buckle of the surcingle under his stomach, so I could finally fix it around him. Practically the whole time, I was holding my breath. This was amazing progress. I was surrounded by mile upon mile of wild country and I was certainly risking my neck, but it seemed the most natural thing in the world. There was this mustang, the open desert and me. I was just beginning to realise the importance of the language of Equus.

He didn't buck. He was 'goosey', but he didn't buck.

I asked him to accept a snaffle bit, and he did so. Later on I was off my saddle horse and working from the ground, putting a stock saddle on him. When he felt the weight of that and when the stirrups were slapping him, he did make an attempt to buck it off, every now and again, for a few seconds at a time. But he wasn't traumatised or overly frightened. I'd asked him to accept quite a number of new experiences that day, and I recognised I wasn't going to be able to ride him until he'd relaxed by a few degrees. I was a long way from help and if I happened to be bucked off and hit one of the stones that littered the ground, the outcome could be catastrophic.

It had been a successful experiment, and I called it a day. I removed the tack and turned him loose.

I was amazed. I could hardly believe that had happened. It was a private, intensely personal relationship between myself and this horse. There was not a soul to witness it and certainly I was dying to tell someone about it. When I returned to the expedition headquarters that year in 1951, I had a conversation with the hired hands there at the Campbell Creek Ranch. I told them what I'd done, hoping they'd realise I was on to something, that this was for real.

They laughed and were incredulous. Their view of it was, that I was a young man who was making up this whole episode out of excessive enthusiasm and a vain desire to promote my abilities. They were jocular but they plain refused to believe it. How many of us would have believed it?

I was determined to come back the next year, in 1952, and I'd be sure to give myself a day or two more time, to see if I could actually ride a mustang back to the ranch. There would be no doubting it then.

Readers of my first book will also remember that I was using this new found technique – which I would call 'join-up' – to start the mustangs at home. After the rodeo had finished, there were around a hundred head which would be sold off, and my brother and I decided to give them some extra value by starting them. My brother 'broke' his share using conventional techniques, but I 'started' mine using join-up. Given this was a good number of horses, I was already beginning to refine my technique in secret, out from under the eyes of my father and others. It was interesting to note how much quicker I had my share of the mustangs up and going than my brother did.

So in 1952, I was better prepared. By now I knew much more about what I was doing and had allowed myself the time necessary to achieve my aim, join-up in the wild, then saddle, bridle and ride him.

I found a strong, bay colt, showing a lot of Andalusian characteristics, high action in front, feathers on his fetlocks and a muscular neck and shoulder. He had large, black eyes with a burning in each of them. Horsemen would say he had an intelligent eye. His entire appearance appealed to me.

As I cut him away from the herd, he was a magnificent sight. He arched his neck, held his nose up and stuck his tail right up in the air so the hair flowed down over his hips. His tail was so long and full that it created a black veil over his haunches down to his hocks.

He cantered away; I followed.

I was struck by his short, powerful stride, so unlike that of the thoroughbred. As I followed, bending him to different directions but essentially driving him away, we settled into a pattern. I knew what to look for, the licking and chewing, the head dipping to ground level. From my experience in the round pen starting all those mustangs after the rodeo last year, my skill at interpreting the language of Equus had increased many fold.

I was quicker. Before twenty-four hours had passed, I could drop a rope around his neck and lead him around. He was very wild, but seemed to be trying hard for me. When I got to the stage of wanting to drop a long-line around his rear quarter – boy, he kicked with a purpose.

Each time he kicked I found myself whispering, 'Hey buster ...', so then he had his name. From that moment I'd refer to him as Buster.

After schooling Buster to get him used to the long lines, I could literally see him decide not to kick. I'd then rub him on the hip bone to congratulate him. The surcingle was on him at around the twenty-four hour mark and he didn't buck. After about thirty hours I was leading him around saddled and bridled. He kicked at the stirrups a few times, but his bucking was limited to a few crow hops, nothing more.

On the afternoon of the third day, I put one foot in the stirrup and lifted my weight on to it. He circled around as I stood there in the stirrup, and it seemed I could swing my leg over and sit on him right then.

However, I wanted to take some precautions. First, I scouted the area on my saddle horse to find a patch with the least stones so if I was to be thrown, I'd be less likely to be injured.

Also, I wore twenty-five feet of rope coiled in my belt, so if I was bucked off, I'd have a chance of holding on to Buster.

On the morning of the fourth day, I rode him.

'Tree Tunnel,' Flag Is Up Farms.

Tuesday morning, a long
day ahead – I hope he accepts
the saddle and bridle.

Preparing for the first
saddle, Monty is putting
on the saddle pad.   93

94   *Approaching with the first saddle.*

Placing first saddle on Shy Boy's back.
This was a very small saddle for
the first step.

95

Left: Allowing Shy Boy the feel of the saddle. Rewarding him for accepting it.

Overleaf: Monty approaching Shy Boy with a western saddle.

97

*Monty putting cinch on
western saddle.*

Monty cinching up western
saddle. Shy Boy is saying
'that tickles.'   *101*

102   *Monty prepares to place the first bit on Shy Boy.*

Above: Just a moment of reflection.

Overleaf: Leading Shy Boy around now, all tacked up.

103

106   *Ready for the ride.*

It was the most amazing feeling. In the middle of the high desert, I'd persuaded this mustang that we were on the same side. There was no round pen, not a fence in sight to contain him. Yet here I was, putting a foot in the stirrup and lifting myself on. The amount of sky and land around me made it doubly exhilarating. We were pinpoints in that huge desert and the sky arched over us, yet I felt we were at the centre of the universe.

Throughout most of that afternoon, I rode Buster. I took care only to ride him for a few minutes at a time and making sure I mounted and dismounted on different sides. I also had him get used to leading my saddle horses.

This was particularly important because it was my intention to ride him back to the ranch headquarters, where a large contingent of cowboys would have it proven to them now that I wasn't making this up. This was for real. I'd gone out into the open country and joined-up with a mustang and rode him back as proof.

It was twenty miles back to the Campbell Creek Ranch headquarters. For most of the way I rode a saddle horse to keep Buster fresh. Then about two miles out from the headquarters, and with no little sense of anticipation, I switched to Buster. I rode him at a trot, leading the other horses. I felt like a million dollars.

Buster marched into the ranch like he'd been doing it all his life. I had to keep an eye on who was going to see me first.

A group of men were doctoring calves in a corral, another few were working on a generator motor over by a barn and a couple of them were coming out of the bunkhouse.

They looked me over and asked, 'What's going on?'

I told them what had happened, expecting to see their expressions change, to have them question me exactly how I'd done this.

Instead there was only scepticism. 'You must have taken an already broken horse and salted the herd,' was one suggestion.

I answered, 'Look at his feet. He's never had a shoe on. You can see he's an out and out mustang.'

Another cowboy spoke up, 'I can see he must have been out there, but you were lucky enough to find one that someone's gotten to first, one that's already broken.'

In just an instant, my morale plummeted. I felt angry and frustrated. This had been a nerve-wracking four days for me. I'd achieved what I thought was a significant breakthrough in the way we deal with horses. Yet, they all thought I was telling tales, making it up.

However, when we returned from the high desert to Salinas without mustangs for that year's rodeo, there were two or three of the hands who were telling people they'd seen me ride in on this mustang, having caused him to accept saddle, bridle and rider in the wild.

And I myself spoke of it as I was determined people should hear about it. I was excited about the potential for this way of working with horses.

Yet everyone squarely put me down. This was a tall tale. It couldn't have happened the way I was suggesting. So I put the whole thing to bed. I would say another word about it to anyone and I'd continue my work in secret for another thirty-five years or so.

Now you know what I was asking these British television people to take on. Anyone would have to view it as a daunting task. All that was almost forty-five years before this moment. It now seemed a faint dream. I was in Britain with a tour to finish. Back to reality.

I completed my engagements, sold the back-up horse Tuffy in Scotland, and flew home. Pat followed with Dually and the equipment a week later, after spending the time waiting for the flight home at Windsor Castle, where Dually, unaware of his privileged state, was stabled down the hall from Her Majesty The Queen's horses.

I told myself to think no more about it.

When I got home to Flag Is Up Farms, there was a message waiting for me from the BBC. If I was willing to try it, they were willing to take the risk and make a programme showing me joining up with a mustang in the wild.

Shy Boy, here I come.

PREPARATION

What the hell was I letting myself in for? I was sixty-two years old. My back was in the poorest state possible, not only having been welded together along five vertebrae, but having the soft inner core of five discs removed. So, could I really ride solid for two days, through thick and thin, night and day, through the wild extremes of temperature you can get in the high desert, dodging the rattlers, the holes in the ground, eating and drinking in the saddle? Could I do all this and still accomplish the goals set for the project – achieving join-up in the wild?

I'd done it before when I was a teenager, and no one had believed it. Now, finally nearly fifty years later, I was being offered the chance to prove I had not made it up, it had happened for real. There wouldn't be any way around it. A film crew would be monitoring my every move. Those guys are experienced documentary producers, their methodology in putting together the programme would ensure there wasn't a single doubt of its authenticity.

There was no way I was going to turn this down. It was do or die. I needed to do it, more than I ever allowed myself to realise. Given the opportunity now, and the funds to mount such an expedition, it brought home to me how much it meant, how much I'd been telling myself to be resigned to the possibility of it never happening. It was the very reason I'd left it out of my first book. I'd told myself not to fuss over something long past, which I could never do again, anyway.

But now, it was all systems go.

Problem number one, the mustang himself. Problem number two, time.

Taking these in order, I'll explain what we had to overcome just to get this idea on the starting blocks.

The mustang, now, is a cultural icon in America and an endangered species. It's part of our heritage. Consequently, and quite properly, the mustang is protected by Federal Law. An Act of Congress forbids anyone interfering with them in any way. They are controlled by the Bureau of Land Management and it's illegal to go near them in their wild state. I told the

BLM what I proposed doing, but they wouldn't hear of it. If they were to stretch the law for me, they'd create a precedent and have to stretch the law for everyone else. They turned me down, flat.

Then, there was the time pressure; when the BBC called it was January. The rattlesnakes come out of hibernation in April, and the risk of fire increases rapidly, so it would have to be before then. Also, I had to plot for some moonlight, so I could have night vision. The ideal time would be the last weekend in March, which happened to be the Easter holiday.

This would have been all right, except for one crucial thing, given the BLM's refusal to treat my expedition as a special case, the only way I could hope to get a hold of a mustang was to adopt one. The BLM runs a system of herd management, whereby a certain number are run off the open range, often using helicopters, and are offered up for adoption to approved homes. The mustangs aren't sold, as this could allow the profit motive to compromise the situation, but names are put into a hat and if you're lucky your name comes up and you can adopt up to four at a time. However, this mustang lottery only happens occasionally, so when I got the news that QED wanted to make the documentary this year, my heart sank. Was there an adoption event soon enough? We'd have to have a whole lot of luck.

At that moment, as God is my judge, one of my students rushed up to me. 'Monty, look, there's an adoption event...'

'When?'

'Tomorrow!'

There was the good luck; we landed on our feet right from the start. It seemed like this was fated to happen. We jumped in the truck and headed to Paso Robles, California.

Now, a mustang that's been captured off the range in this way is no less wild, in fact, rather the opposite. His adrenaline would be sky high. The whole experience would have put him in full flight mode and he'd be less easy to settle. I'd have a less wild mustang if I'd been allowed to cut one out of a feral herd on his home territory.

I was after males, not females because they were likely to be pregnant. I wanted three males, a first choice, as good-looking as possible for the cameras, and then a back-up, and a second back-up. And I wanted all of them aged three to four years old.

Among the 220 head up for adoption, only twenty fitted into this category.

We put our names in a hat along with fifty-five other people who were going to be lucky enough that day to be offered the chance to adopt.

Once more, the prospects of the whole enterprise hinged on fate. In short, we needed more luck.

We waited, my students and myself, while the names were called.

At number forty-nine, mine hadn't been called. Fifty-one, and I still wasn't mentioned. I was going to have to go home and tell them to cancel the shoot.

The very last name out of the hat was mine. Our luck held, having been a hair's breadth from failure.

The next piece of luck we needed was to secure the mustangs from that group of twenty identified as male and the right age. I look around the wild mustangs corralled there in Paso Robles, and one in particular caught my eye. He was more handsome than all the rest. He had a brighter spark in his eye and he moved to avoid all human contact quicker and more fiercely than the others. I could see in his build, in the way he carried himself, the classic Spanish ancestry. Proud, strong heritage of his forefathers, developed to a high degree.

He was looking at me out of the corner of his eye and he didn't want anything to do with me. It was like he was saying, 'Stay away. I'm wild as hell and I'm going to stay that way. I don't know what's going on here, this is outside my experience, but I sure as hell don't want to find out.' I could see immediately that here was a character to contend with, but equally a character that anyone would be proud to get acquainted with.

This was Shy Boy. I didn't have his name yet, but we were about to start a relationship as close as any I've had with a wild horse.

I made a note of the number tag he wore, then I moved on to identify the back-up horses and wrote down two further numbers. Given I was the last name, I'd be lucky if any was still available when it came my turn.

Again, our luck held, and I got the mustangs I wanted. I had the feeling now that this was meant to happen. We'd had three straight hits of good luck, one after the other. Someone was watching over me. I was meant to do this. Maybe it had even been intended that I should have to wait this long to prove myself, because now I could do it with a film crew proving it to the world.

My three youngsters were run down the chute, unknowingly adopted for this unique project. The more I looked at Shy Boy, the more I noticed how he was a couple of steps ahead of the others in the style of his movement, the personality and intelligence in his eye. I was pleased to have him.

Back home at Flag Is Up, the mustangs entered the environment of the domestic horse. They were worried, confused. When they heard the sounds of other horses calling out to one another, they ran to a corner of their enclosure and huddled together, lowered their heads and walked as stealthily as possible. In their view, the domestic horses were breaking the rules; they were attracting predators from miles around with their unnecessary calling. I'd witnessed this phenomenon may times before, but it was interesting for my students to see first hand the difference in the culture of the wild horses.

My first concern, I have to say, was to get Shy Boy away from there. I did not want him to be around people and I certainly didn't want him to be around me. I'd discussed the measures we ought to take to ensure that people could know we were dealing with a wild horse, given that the only way to get hold of one was this adoption process. We came up with the plan of attaching a referee, who would continually monitor the mustangs from now until the start of the project, to ensure there was objective proof they remained untouched and away from human contact.

Therefore, a woman by the name of Carol Childerley, sometimes associated with the Santa Barbara Wildwatch Association, took charge of all three mustangs from that point. She made arrangements to transport them up to the high desert to be mixed with a privately owned feral herd on a ranch of thousands of acres. She would check them regularly to confirm they weren't handled and their status hadn't changed.

Of course, once mustangs have been adopted, they can't go back on to land owned by the BLM. The adoption charter requires they be kept on private lands, so this ranch we had the good fortune to be using was intended to be as near as possible their natural habitat. The only reminder it wasn't virgin territory was that there were fences every twelve miles or so.

Now we had recruited Shy Boy, I felt our major organisational difficulties were over. We had our mustang, and two back-ups should anything go wrong with him. All we had to do now was to prepare our saddle horses and equipment and wait for Easter Sunday.

AGAINST CRUELTY

It's worth bearing in mind at this point, that my whole attitude in dealing with horses has been an effort to go in the opposite direction from cruelty. This ambition on my part was triggered by two main experiences. Firstly, watching the methods used by my father – and many, many others – in forcing horses into submission, tying up their legs and all that goes with the traditional methods. Secondly, witnessing my father beating that black man in 1943. These two elements, together with the physical abuse I suffered at the hands of my father, have created the personality that I am. I felt my character change as a result of them.

Perhaps it's no accident that my demonstrations are an effective focus for those members of the audience who themselves have suffered physical abuse. It's been an unexpected but rewarding side to the demonstrations to find some members of the audience who undergo a more intense and personal emotional catharsis on observing what I do and why. As far as I know, all those who've fainted at my demonstrations have suffered sexual or physical abuse. Consequently, as well as showing people the language of Equus, I've found myself often privileged to hear private confessions on human experience, and sometimes I've had the opportunity to be of some help.

Domestic abuse, I've learned, is more prevalent than I ever thought. If there are 2,000 people in the building for a demonstration, between 600 and a 1000 people will come and talk to me during one of the three sessions provided (three and one half hours). Of this number that I talk to, there will be some twenty to thirty who experience physical abuse in their own family and often they'll be pleased they have managed to talk about it. It's not easy.

There must be the same number again, and probably the worst cases, who avoid at all costs talking about it, and for good reason. To talk about it can break families apart. But, in my opinion, to resort to cruelty and violence should never be the way things are done. To beat a child is never the answer. Abuse is always destructive. Some young people recover, but for many the damage is irreversible, just as it can be in animals, also.

Landscape in California.

First attempt to mount, Shy Boy

saying, 'Are you kidding? Not a chance.'

Second attempt successful. This is actually
in the first minute of riding.

Congratulations
all-round.

Left: On a morning after, two friends reflecting on victory over a major challenge.

Above: Monty, Dually and Shy Boy observing the spring-blooming yucca plants on top of the mountain.

121

Monty, Dually and Shy Boy
enjoying the California
landscape.   123

Monty reaching out to Shy Boy to give reward.

*Monty, Dually and Shy Boy, a
moment in the mountain.*

Above: Christian Bunneman looking
out over the high desert.

Overleaf: "New York City' Matt and T.J.
at the Riverdale Equestrian Center.

130   *Old sceptics – new believers.*

It has not been a comfortable experience bringing my life story out in print. I suppose there is a price to be paid for speaking out. My relatives' denial of certain facts in my past, of which they can know nothing since they weren't there, is nothing less than their effort at creating their own family history. My account of my father threatens their lineage, their reputations. It's an ongoing attempt on their part to preserve what they perceive to be their right to be violent.

In my mind, I am glad that I have published my books. Not to talk about these things is to disguise them at least and, at the worst, to condone them. By sharing them, I hope I have helped both people and animals.

Perhaps the most dramatic case of someone speaking for the first time of physical abuse at one of my demonstrations occurred recently on the first American tour we did, to coincide with the publication in the USA.

MEMPHIS COWBOY

We were on tour just outside an American city, one of those stops where we were to do two demonstrations on successive nights. I was half way through the first evening.

There were nearly 2,000 people in the audience and it seemed as though each one had at least two or three items for me to sign. I noticed a huge man in the line. He had a red face and while he wasn't much over forty, the sun had made its marks, leaving fissures on the skin tanned to the texture of leather. He wore a meticulously creased cowboy hat that had obviously seen a few seasons of hard work, but held its shape so as to tell a story not only of its own quality but also to attest to the fact that he was a pro and proud of it. Years of dressing motion picture actors in an attempt to make them look authentic had taught me how difficult it is for a lay person to achieve 'the look'.

When he was a dozen or so people from reaching me, he stepped slightly out of line, maybe it was subconscious, but nevertheless it allowed me to see that his shirt, Wrangler blue jeans and his boots were all correct for a top cowboy. He faced squarely on me just before returning to the line giving me a chance to see a trophy buckle with a few years on it and obviously earned in rodeo competition. Once you are a professional cowboy, it is never hard to spot another, and I had many years in which to imprint that image on my brain. They don't often get in a line for anything, these cowboys, least of all for someone's autograph. The curiosity in me heightened as he worked his way to the front. Maybe he'll say he rodeoed with me at some point, I thought. This sort of thing happens quite often. Maybe he'll remind me of an old friendship we once had. Maybe he won't want my autograph at all, say he's a professional 'horse breaker' and that my work is a load of rubbish. This too has happened.

'I want to thank you, Mr Roberts. I've really learned something tonight. I don't have a book. All I have is this little piece of paper that I'd like you to sign, but that's not really important. I would have stood in this line for two more hours just to shake your hand.'

With that he put a hand across the top of my signing table that looked as though it could have crushed stones for a living. I have big hands and they're strong, too. Be he had enormous hands and the thickness of them was awesome. His demeanour, though, caused me to willingly put my signing hand into that reddish freckled vice and allow him to squeeze out its appreciation for what he had seen. I will never forget how he looked me in the eye and said, 'You taught me something tonight, something I don't believe any other man could. I'm going to get your book. I might even see you tomorrow night.'

As he walked away, I realised that he was alone in that line. It's something that cowboys would almost never do. Being alone is okay when you're working on the ranch, but when you come to town, you just don't line up with a bunch of city folk without a couple of ranch hands for company. I must have signed for another hour or so, but I hardly got him out of my mind.

The following night's event got started routinely and I finished up in an ordinary fashion. I was on the signing stand and I suddenly realised that my friend was standing out to my left about two yards in an open uncrowded area. At least six foot four inches tall and built even stronger than I remembered, he stood about two yards from four little girls. They were all in dresses and each with long red curls down their backs. I would guess them to be between the ages of eight and eleven, but I recall remarking to myself that they were as cute as could be. He stood with a book in one hand and a look on his face much like the night before, stern and studious. When the line had reduced itself to a couple of people, he came walking toward my stand, to the side of it, not straight up to the front door. I winced a bit at the thought of another handshake, but I braced for it because I was happy to see he had returned.

'I read your book since I saw you last night,' he said, 'the whole thing. I never slept. Don't read too fast either. Never read another book clear through in my whole life. You've done good things, Mr Roberts. You're bringing good things to horses. I'll never treat horses the same again. My father was brutal to them, too, just like yours. But you know what I've got to say to that? To hell with the horses. What I want to know is, is it too late for

133

those four little girls over there?' With that he began to sob. I put an arm around his hulking frame and escorted him to a horse trailer nearby. We achieved a small amount of protection from those who would be staring.

The little girls came slowly along, maintaining eight or ten yards between us. They waited huddled together while their father related stories of his brutality to horses, those little girls and their mother as well. He said that his wife just couldn't come along. She feared too much what he was going through. He said that he thought she felt safer at home. He admitted to being arrested on two separate occasions, the result of friends turning him in, but said that his wife denied being beaten and got the charges dropped. He told me that his wife had covered for him on one occasion when he was questioned about reports that the girls had been severely beaten. With his arms around me, he pleaded for help and with assistance to locate an agency in his community. He is now under their care and counselling and at the last report he is doing quite well.

Before leaving me that night, he held the four little girls in two massive arms and pleaded for their forgiveness. He promised never to mistreat them again and asked them to please tell their mother what he had said. If this particular evening was all that I ever got for a lifetime of work, it would be worth it to me. My hand is now back to normal and I'm signing away as usual.

THE HIGH DESERT

The Cuyama Valley lies between the Sierra Madre and the Caliente range in California. Geologically it is an area of exceptional interest. At its eastern end is the San Andreas Fault, which at that point changes its direction about twenty-five degrees to a more north-westerly orientation. Because of this, the mountains are being twisted in a counter-clockwise direction and at the same time being flipped over. It sounds perilous, but of course there's neither sight nor sound of this movement. Mostly, it's a civilised if complicated gyration of the earth's crust, except for the occasional earthquake.

The Cuyama Valley therefore sits up there in what's known as a transverse range, a mountain range running east to west, between the dominant ranges running north to south. It's drier because it sees many more hours of sun. The ground is a combination of granite and sandstone, quartz, feldspar and fine loam. I personally can only see in black and white, but I've been told for those of you colour-sighted, there's a wide variety from ochre, burnt orange, slate grey, chalk and cream. The high desert flora is there, also. Yucca is a particular favourite of mine. It flowers annually with a white, almost luminous bloom held high on a stem making it easy to be pollinated by moths in the moonlight. It's known as 'desert candle'.

Way up here, in the Cuyama Valley, Shy Boy was taken, along with his two back-up mustangs. They joined the privately owned feral herds. Carol Childerley would go there regularly, to check that Shy Boy and the other mustangs were okay.

It is as similar to the natural mustang ranges as is possible to find. Thousands of acres, a fence every twelve miles or so, we were in the wild. I was ready to prove to myself, as well as to the world at large, that I could do now what I did back then in the early fifties, and achieve join-up out here without a round pen in sight – just myself, the mustang, the ground under our feet and the big sky over us.

I would have three of my horses with me for this task. Dually, of course, would be there, schooled so precisely that his movements can be perfectly judged to within an inch with the lightest of touches. I would use him for the last stage, for join-up, when I'd need to imitate with accuracy the stance and movements of a matriarch of the wild herd. Furthermore, I had a dark, handsome horse called The Cadet, a ranch horse type with a big trot on him – he trots at around twelve and one half miles an hour. I felt he would be useful when things were settled down after I'd first cut Shy Boy from his adoptive herd. Thirdly, I had Big Red Fox, a tall bay, a nine-year-old retired racehorse. He seemed to me very fit for the job, and in a curious way, so it would prove.

The plan was to use The Cadet to cut Shy Boy from the herd, then at dusk switch to Big Red Fox for the moonlit period, during which we'd be allowing Shy Boy to rest and eat. Some time the next morning, I'd switch to Dually for the delicate, highly charged moments of join-up.

All three horses had very fit cardio-vascular systems. I myself had done a lot of trotting, around three to five miles a day, to get my fitness up to a decent level.

The ropes, saddles, tents and the entire equipment list for the expedition had been collected, gone over and rechecked dozens of times.

Five ranch hands were available to me, one of them Caleb Twissleman, a sixteen-year-old boy who was to shadow me personally and the other four, including Cathy Twissleman, Caleb's mother, were to take Shy Boy's adoptive feral herd off in the other direction once we'd cut him out.

We'd arranged a base camp for the expedition in a very particular location. It was high atop a hill in the centre of the thousands of acres allocated. It happened to be near the best of the grazing areas which would be helpful when allowing Shy Boy some grazing time.

This base camp had to look after quite a population, because, of course, there would be the television crew to feed as well as the wranglers and various other assistants.

Then, we had a warning; the rattlesnakes had come out early. They strike at body heat and when they first emerge from their dark winter dens, they're cranky and unpredictable, a disaster waiting to happen.

The film shoot actually began Saturday, the 29th of March, and not with a beautiful dawn and a wild mustang in flight across an incredible landscape … but instead in the Maverick Saloon, Santa Ynez, where there was line dancing to Art Green's band. The film crew was happy to find old-timer, Dutch Wilson telling anyone who'd listen in his wonderful drawl, 'Maunteee's absolutely crazeee. He stands as good a chance as any, of being killed outright … so who is it wants to go with him?'

Others joined in. 'You want my opinion'? It's not going to be easy. Lot of people bin' killed, tryin' to break mustangs.'

'Tell you something about mustangs. The most dangerous part of him is his front feet. His back feel will hurt you, but his front feet will kill ya!'

'You see a lot of cowboys round here with broken teeth.'

'And the bones to go with 'em.'

This didn't put me off. I felt relaxed and as ready as I ever would be. My thinking at this point was, that if I were to fail to accomplish my dream now, it wouldn't be because I hadn't had a chance at it.

I left the Maverick Saloon at around nine o'clock and drove for approximately an hour and a half to the high desert. There I slept in my trailer for a few hours. It was bitterly cold, a warning of what I'd have to put up with the following night when I was out there alone with no camp. But, the thought occurred, the cold would keep the rattlers asleep a while longer.

Then, it was daylight, Easter Sunday. Yes, it had almost a religious significance. It was my time in the wilderness. The difference was, I was expected to come out the other end with something very definite to show everyone.

The first thing I did was to stick on to the insides of my knees, thighs and calves a membrane made by 3M, which I'd discovered. It's like a second skin and it's used by marathon runners for protection against blisters. Over this tape I pulled on long-johns, trousers and chaps. I was prepared to ride for a day, a night and then probably most of the day as well. For my bad back, I was on anti-inflammatory tablets and, of course, I was strapped into a back brace. To protect myself against cold, I had five layers of clothing on, although this would still leave my hands and face exposed.

At first light the ranch hands had gathered to move the cattle off to clear the area and leave it open for the horses. Last-minute adjustments were made as to who was riding what horse, and then we set out from headquarters moving west alongside the river. My group consisted of Pat Russell, Cathy and Caleb Twissleman, Barney Skelton, Scott Silvera and myself. Somewhere out there, Shy Boy was waiting for us.

This is big country, in every sense of the word. It's where they come to make the Marlboro cigarette ads. The early sun brought the place alive, I noticed the white hives for the bees which feed off sage. Sycamores lined the river beds in the alleys; yucca and cactus grew in abundance.

We met up with the feral horses more or less where we expected to, around a mile from the headquarters. Shy Boy was there, his head high, one of the crowd to observe our approach, yet he stood out because of his looks and his enquiring nature. By the look of it, he was more or less assimilated into his new family. He was lean, fit, in prime condition. Keeping my eye on him, I marvelled that he had no idea what was about to happen, the amount of resources which had been expended in this bid to see him getting a gentle start, a film director and crew, a helicopter, no less and a whole wrangling operation, here. It was amazing. There was a special light in his eye, did he have some idea he was in for an experience or two?

There was also a veterinarian and animal behaviourist, Dr Robert Miller, to observe and comment for the camera on what I was doing. He also was there to certify that Shy Boy was as wild as a deer and to give his seal of approval that there was no cruelty involved in the treatment of any animal on the shoot from the lowliest pack horse right up to Shy Boy himself.

Carol Childerley who had been in charge of the three mustangs for nearly two months now was on the scene to verify that Shy Boy was the same wild unhandled mustang that had been adopted in Paso Robles nearly sixty days prior. She carefully observed his movements and reported that he was a bona fide wild horse as pure as any you could find.

Christopher Dydyk took up a position just behind the film crew and with tripods, a Hasselblad and lenses looking like stovepipes was prepared to

138

*Above: Monty and Dually looking out
across the high desert.*

*Overleaf: Shy Boy enjoying a wild
gallop on a spring morning.*

Above: A casual canter.

Right: Shy Boy and Caleb ready to round up cattle.

144   *Cathie Twissleman.*

146   *Tree sculpture on the high desert.*

Above: More civilized, near Flag Is Up.

Overleaf: Caleb on Shy Boy and Monty on The Cadet during the round-up.

Left: Zane Davis before the round-up on Arnie.

Above: Caleb and Shy Boy bringing some cattle in.

Overleaf: Monty on The Cadet watching Shy Boy work.

*Previous page (top): Cathie Twissleman
and Pat Roberts also watching
Shy Boy at work.*

*Previous page (bottom): Caleb and
Shy Boy 'flying' over the ground.*

154   *Above: Dually at work.*

document the event with still photos. What he did can be seen by the marvellous works of art chronicling this adventure as seen on these pages.

The film crew moved into place.

I gave my instructions: the six of us would ride into the herd and Caleb and I would cut Shy Boy to take him east towards the open country. I knew he would live up to his forebears. He was a true mustang and I knew he'd fly when he felt himself alone away from the herd. He'd be in full flight and I'd have a job to keep up with him. Caleb would follow me leading a pack horse. The others meanwhile would muster the rest of the herd and keep them going in the opposite direction, west. It was best if they were out of the way as soon as possible. I didn't want Shy Boy to feel any pull towards them. I wanted them out of sight and mind.

We rode in and split them like a bunch of snooker balls and suddenly it was working. The herd was off in one direction and I was driving Shy Boy in full flight over the high desert the other way . The film from the helicopter shows a sleek, fast mustang, fluent and youthful, followed by a well-padded old cowboy galloping behind him. Shy Boy's vigour, strength, innocence, as well as that spirited element to his character, were now all the more evident alongside my precarious strength as well as infirmities age will bring on. What I had going for me was my experience with horses.

In terms of the round pen this would equate to my sending the horse round the ring, causing him to go into flight. In terms of the psychology of the wild herd, I was the dominant mare running at the adolescent, driving it away to show I was displeased and asking it to show me some respect.

But I hadn't reckoned on the level of panic induced by the helicopter. Mustangs are regularly driven and captured in the wild by aircraft so they're scared of them and Shy Boy was no exception. I had to wave the helicopter back some distance away if this horse wasn't going to be run into the ground. It was no easy task trying to signal the helicopter while using a radio tied to your saddle bags at full gallop.

A lot of the time I had to be up out of the saddle, standing in the stirrups, to save The Cadet's back. This was very demanding for a man of sixty-two

_155_

with a welded spine. I was unsure of the ground and a fall at that speed could have been fatal.

Eventually the helicopter got the message and stayed further back. We eased off to a workable pace.

No sooner had this happened than we faced another challenge. We'd covered nearly twelve miles and were heading towards the first fence. This would be a barbed wire cattle fence and it would be dangerous to Shy Boy if he came into contact with it. When they're in flight like this, wild mustangs don't see fences so well. It was critically important to keep this mustang as safe as possible. Not only did I feel a strong need to protect him, because of all that I stand for, but it was extremely important to keep him safe and sound for the completion of this project.

The task was to circle his flank and head him off. I picked up the pace, and moving at a slight angle, I managed to bend him around well short of the fence.

That afternoon, Shy Boy led me to every single water hole, stream and cattle trough. It reminded me of how good mustangs are at finding water in the wild. They have an uncanny ability for it in their high desert with its long dry spells.

There were areas of an acre or so where ground squirrels would burrow and I could watch Shy Boy skip around these holes barely breaking step. I had to be very careful indeed not to put The Cadet straight into one of them and cause a fall.

As I was riding I pulled beef jerky from my bag and sipped water from the canteen. I talked to myself and to Shy Boy encouraging us both to keep going. It was one hell of a ride.

Towards the end of the daylight hours things settled. We slowed dramatically. It wasn't my intention to pursue him through the night, only to follow, keeping tabs on him. Shy Boy needed to rest and to eat and drink. As for that, so did I. More than ever in my life.

I'd been riding at this point for seven or eight hours at a fairly good clip. The Cadet also had to rest, especially given that the helicopter had pushed us on more than I would have liked. We had counted on the strength and fitness of both Shy Boy and The Cadet, and we'd come through phase one.

Now for the tricky part: night.

Caleb Twissleman drew up alongside and handed over my night-time horse, Big Red Fox. He took The Cadet back to the camp and gave him over to my wife, Pat, who groomed, fed and watered him. She bandaged his legs with poultices to keep any heat from building up and gave him electrolytes to replenish his fluids.

I watched Shy Boy take on water and graze. He'd keep an eye on me and occasionally quickly move off, but then I'd trail him. He was disconcerted, asking me for an explanation. But he wasn't asking to join-up with me. Not yet.

It began to get darker.

Shy Boy slowed and I was pleased to let him. I began to watch him more closely, assessing his character; what sort of animal was this? From his response to me during these last minutes of dusk, I judged him to have an impish quality, a spring to his stride that added to his attraction.

The mustang became Shy Boy to me and ultimately the rest of the world on the night of March 30th, 1997. I was in the high desert wilderness of central California attempting to prove to the world what I had done forty-five years previously. The moon lit our private world out there. No one else was in sight. It was these two horses, one domestic and one wild, and myself.

That night, as I rode in Shy Boy's wake, I felt a kinship – if not yet with him, then with his kind. We shared, in a way, a dark past. Those of his ancestors who had escaped slaughterhouse trucks earlier this century were conscripted as war horses or ranch horses – but only after being savagely broken. I was no stranger to that cruelty, to horses, or men.

By midnight or so, Shy Boy had filled himself with good grass and seemed to assume a more relaxed and restful attitude. I was happy to oblige him and relieve Big Red Fox of my weight. The three of us could rest for fifteen minute stretches.

It was a magical experience. I was in the high desert, miles from everyone, following my dream, a dream that I had held for forty-five years. I was standing in the middle of it now. It was a dream, and yet it was real. I had to pinch myself on occasions as a reminder of the reality that surrounded me. I was there and the horses were, too, allowing me to prove what really happened so long ago.

Of course, during this long cold night memories cam back to me. I recalled a time when, as a teenager, I was employed at night to gather some wild cattle on a neighbouring ranch, and the horse I was riding literally galloped over an unseen cliff and flew through the darkness. Luckily at the bottom where we had landed it was sandy and neither the horse nor I was injured.

Another strange memory was of spending the night in jail, at the invitation of the sheriff. It was the only bed available apart from the brothel. It was in this little one-horse town where I was unlucky enough to have had my brand new vehicle catch fire as I was driving along.

A similarly cold, uncomfortable night was spent, two or three of them in fact, when I was hiding out in the hills above Santa Ynez Valley. My family's and my farm's existence were threatened by a man with severe psychological disorders who took it into his head to try and destroy me. Those few nights were cold and uncomfortable, but much worse, they were filled with doubt, anxiety and fear of failure.

I was tired from being in the saddle for eighteen hours, but so long as Big Red Fox, with this magical gift he had, could keep track of this mustang in the misty darkness, I was still hopeful for success.

Around four thirty a.m. there was just a glow of light in the eastern sky. With the first hint of sun up, I noticed a quickening in Shy Boy's tempo. As the glow was turned up and progressed toward dawn, the pace picked up still more. Shy Boy was up to a trot. Luckily the fog was gone and I could see him easier now. Big Red Fox kept him in his sights. This sturdy horse was flawless in his fitness and he'd proved uncannily suitable for the slot we'd chosen for him.

Shy Boy's head was high and thrust forward drinking in the smells of a new day. He seemed to be headed for the now slightly lit rim of the world. He was off to my right about one hundred yards and east; we went at a canter. Once more I had to grasp the saddle horn and raise my weight off Foxy's back. It was then that I realised that I had massive blisters across my fingers from the day before. I was frightened as it seemed we were destined to go forever. I had begun at this point to see the bottom of my endurance and, if it hadn't been for the brilliance and generosity of Big Red Fox, I'm not sure I would have made it.

It was after five a.m. and still in dim light, when Shy Boy settled back to a reasonable pace and I was able to encourage him to bend to a westerly direction toward the camp. Trotting comfortably now, I was about to use my radio to alert Pat and Caleb that a change of horses was in order. My nose and ears were icicles as the three of us approached an area just to the north of the base camp where I spotted Pat and Dually on the ridge off to my right.

I'd been riding for nearly twenty-four hours non-stop, but I kept upright in the saddle.

Then, we suddenly found ourselves riding right through base camp. Was this Shy Boy's sense of humour? Was he aiming to take me back to my species, since I must have looked to him as if I had had all I could handle of the wilderness?

Shy Boy, I would later learn, wanted water and there was a trough north of the camp. The fact that he had come so close to camp en route was proof of a dramatic change in demeanour: he was still wary of people and trucks, but he seemed possessed of a new calm. It was as if he had waltzed into the kitchen.

My daughter, Laurel, told me later they were all amazed when they first saw Shy Boy appear from over the hill, and then the top of my hat. She and Christopher had been discussing the difficulties I must have faced with the fog. The weather and tension had clearly affected them all.

Quite a cheer went up as first Shy Boy and then I rode over the brow of the hill still firmly glued to the saddle. Laurel shouted out to me, 'You look like hell, Dad.' I growled back, 'I feel like hell.'

I didn't know it, but my face was black, caked with sweat and dust. The wind had flattened my hat brim right back to its crown. Laurel ran alongside and give me a Diet Coke and a piece of beef jerky. I gladly took them from her.

I caught sight of my wife, Pat, and our eyes locked for a few moments. I saw her eyes fill with emotion and I felt the same. I'd come through the night. I'd survived the freezing fog.

Then I heard Pat call out, 'Monty, are you all right? Can you make it?' It was then that I came to focus on how near failure I really was. And now it was time to reach back for that extra ingredient that success demands.

As I left camp, I could hear their voices raised in excitement, dwindling behind me. It had been a morale booster this contact with my family and crew after the uncertainty and isolation of the night. It was around five thirty in the morning in the dimmest of light, and I could see the headlights of the television vehicles which were kicking up dust on the dirt road a couple of miles east of the camp.

The director's voice crackled to life on the walkie-talkie and I was able to tell him we were running according to schedule. I'd been in the saddle for twenty-four hours but still on course with Shy Boy in sight. I gave him a fix on my position so he could do any filming he wanted. We were a slow trot now and Shy Boy was taking me to the north where there was a water trough. I stood off about fifty yards as Shy Boy lowered his muzzle into the large galvanised steel container, around a yard deep and two by four yards in size.

I waited.

Then, I waited some more. Unless he was going to drink the whole tank, something wasn't quite right.

I edged closer and Shy Boy headed off, but no water dripped from his mouth. As I came up to the tank, I could see why. A thick layer of ice covered the surface. It had been super cold.

Apparently I'd been out there in temperatures down to minus eight degrees centigrade. I dismounted and took a fencing tool from my saddle bag and broke a large hole in the ice so that both horses could drink. Big Red Fox took his fill and then we stood well back to allow Shy Boy his turn. He wandered to the trough keeping his usual wary eye on us, and as he drank I had time to reflect on the night I had just come through. I will never forget the beauty of it, the shadows at dusk allowing me to see deep dark silhouettes of the mountains on all sides and a moon hanging there just for a 'night light', Hale Bopp coming by providing a magnificent meteoric light show for Shy Boy, Foxy and me, the Pacific ocean sending up a misty veil to add to the wonderment of it all, and Big Red Fox guiding me like a heat-sensing missile ever onward toward the only true object in my life throughout the duration of this event.

And then there were those things which were not so positive, but 'ever burned' into my memory, the extreme cold accompanied by driving winds that seemed to turn my clothing inside out and reach my skin with relentless accuracy, the holes in the ground that chilled my blood but seemed no obstacle for a pair of wonderful equine athletes, the blisters on my hands and a back that was now screaming for a few hours of rest.

On balance the positive outweighed the negatives by a ton. It was after six by now and the sun was pushing the darkness across the horizon and I could see the crew setting up their cameras about a quarter of a mile to the west of me. I felt a surge start in my toes and go quickly to the top of my brain. I think this is what they call a second wind. I was excited now. I got the sense that the worst of it was over.

I watched Shy Boy flicking his nose on the surface of the water as if to say to it how much he loved it and how he always wanted some of it to be within his reach. A term went through my mind at that point in time, 'catastrophic bonding'. I learned about it in psychology classes. It's the same sort of thing that happens to surviving plane crash victims spending hours together on the top of the mountain. Coming through something together that calls on the ultimate in inner strength often causes a friendship everlasting.

It was obvious that Shy Boy still wasn't all that convinced that I was worth that kind of commitment, but I was certainly on my way to reaching that feeling for him.

After Shy Boy had grazed a bit, we started work again. The cameras were once more recording our every move. By eight o'clock I found I could square up to him, look him in the eye and cause him to stop. Then I'd pull up, break off eye contact and rein Big Red Fox away from him. We were entering into the join-up phase.

The mustang had learned that flight wasn't going to work. He was going to have to deal with me. He was going to have to ask for my help and enter into a dialogue. It was just up to me to listen, to ready the signals and to show that I understood his language by the speed and accuracy of my response.

At this point I needed Dually. I felt I was no more than an hour or two away from join-up and I wanted the precision trained horse to be able to make the accurate movements necessary to complete join-up effectively. I squeezed the button of the walkie-talkie and asked Caleb to bring me Dually.

We made the change over and Big Red Fox was taken back for his well-earned rest. He'd been a godsend, that horse. I was as proud of him as the parent of an honour student would be. An honour student is exactly what he had been. He'd gone to class, quickly learned his lessons and passed all tests with flying colours. I was particularly happy to know that he had come through the night free of any physical problems.

Dually, of course, was fresh and to begin with he was a bit playful. He wanted to buck and fool around, so to speak. Shy Boy I could see, was put out with the exuberance of this new horse. It was a good fifteen or twenty minutes before things settled down.

Now I could speak the language of Equus.

This mustang could put an ear on me, lower his nose and in the same instant I'd have Dually break away, retreat from him and let him off the hook. The minute the mustang changed his idea and started going away, wham! we were on him, advancing, becoming the aggressor, which in his language would promote relaxation, return and co-operation.

The cameras were rolling. I was ecstatic. Experience has taught me that after achieving this level of communication the outcome was almost certainly success. After twenty-four hours, a forty-five year old episode from my life was being played out and I felt an intensity of achievement that I had rarely felt in my life.

*A glorious spring sky contrasting
with the dark desert mountain.*

Above: Pat showing her pleasure, watching Dually and Monty in the cutting pen.

Opposite: Shy Boy and Caleb looking for cattle across the canyon.

*Above: There's the herd and Shy Boy
sees them.*

*Opposite: Dr Robert Miller, veterinarian,
watching over the entire project.*

Shy Boy's gone and it
doesn't look good.

Overleaf: Attempting
to bring him back with
a silent prayer, Monty
is thinking perhaps
he shouldn't have let
him go.

169

*Previous page: In the morning light, now
what do we see?*

Above: Shy Boy returns directly to Monty.

Opposite: Monty and Pat heading home
174 *after a successful venture.*

Caleb's little sister, Tara, gets a kiss from Shy Boy after his return.

176

Above: For her latest sculpture
Pat Roberts takes a measurement
from Shy Boy...

Right: And this is the result: a
masterpiece!

178

Within another forty-five minutes, I could walk in circles around Shy Boy and have him bend to follow me. Instead of me following him all over those acres, he was slowly following me to show that he trusted me.

We were on our way. I sent out a very strong silent message to the rattle-snakes, 'Please stay asleep.'

At ten a.m. I asked Caleb over the radio if he would come up and take part by approaching the other side of Shy Boy. Caleb came promptly and was there across from me to help stabilise Shy Boy while I went through the routine of touching and rubbing him for the first time.

This was it. I leaned over the saddle horn and rubbed his neck, a man and a horse in an awesome landscape, connected for the first time. It was a powerful moment. I told him how nice he was to decide to be with me, no ropes, no pain, no fear. It was a remarkable feeling.

Dr Robert Miller agreed. As he said, 'This is an animal that could kick a fly off the wall. Yet, of his own free will, he is accepting a human touch.' For me, this was a privilege.

At the same time as this happened, I experienced simultaneous triumph and exhaustion. Certain phrases began to explode in my brain as if announced by a messenger. 'I am alive. I'm relatively okay. I'm riding Dually. I've completed twenty-six hours in the saddle. I've got a mustang standing with me. I've achieved join-up. I've proven I did do it, all those years ago...'

These announcements ringing in my brain were accompanied by a sensation of happiness and satisfaction difficult to quantify. They immediately ranked alongside those landmark incidents which have meant the most to me in my life, our marriage, the births of three children, the day I turned away from my father's traditional ways and the first time I saw my world champion horse, Johnny Tivio.

It occurred to me that this would be just such a pivotal moment so long as we managed to get on and ride him.

I felt a surge of renewed energy.

The next step was to drop a loose rope around his neck and school him to lead alongside Dually.

He didn't like this new idea. But when he went into flight, I didn't try to stop him. On the contrary, I agreed with him. 'Go on, run away, but don't run a little, run a lot.' I drove him away until he was asking to come back. It didn't take long until he trusted me and was leading comfortably.

Most of that morning was taken up with join-up, putting the rope on him and leading him with Dually.

Then came a bit of rest and a bite to eat. The animals were allowed to graze. Cathy Twissleman was delegated to watch Shy Boy and she reported that he showed no sign of flight. He was content to remain near the domestic horses.

In the afternoon I swapped Dually for George, a solid ranch horse. We spent most of the afternoon schooling Shy Boy in big circles leading him from George. Once in awhile a spark would ignite and Shy Boy would spook and blast away, but his periods of trust and co-operation were lengthening steadily.

George was great. He was thick with a low centre of gravity which made it easy to rub Shy Boy over the back, ribs and hips. Shy Boy quickly became comfortable with George and I was pleased at how that allowed me to massage Shy Boy from head to hip and wither to brisket.

At around four in the afternoon I decided that we had progressed far enough for me to put a surcingle on Shy Boy. I remained on George, slid the surcingle down the offside of Shy Boy, and used a wire hook to catch the buckle beneath him, bringing the girth up to the near side. Shy Boy took the girthing without a complaint; he did not buck or even jump. He never kicked at me, although he did strike out once or twice with his front feet when I moved too quickly for him.

After the surcingle I decided that he had had enough for one day and I felt it was certain that we were safe to get a night's rest. We'd achieved join-up and we were well on the way to putting a saddle and bridle on him.

You might say I needed a night's sleep at this point, maybe more than at any time in my life. I'd been up for thirty-six hours and completed some of the most arduous riding I'd encountered in my entire career. I was exhausted. Strangely though, I had gotten the most remarkable second wind and it was hard to come down from that natural high. I've had a lifetime of athletic activity of one sort or another, but I've never enjoyed a second wind like I did that day. The major contributor it seemed was the moment of join-up. Before that I had felt so tired I was frightened that I might black out. Join-up seemed to give me a surge of energy, excitement and fuel that carried me for the rest of the day.

It was no minor miracle that my back stayed together through this thirty-six hours and I shall be eternally grateful to whatever force allowed this bonus.

Pat helped me take the 3M patches off my legs and miraculously the skin was all there and in surprisingly good shape.

All the horses were fed and watered in one particular area close to the main camp and the crew divided up the night watch duties.

I was excused of any night duties, had some welcome nourishment and crashed. I slept like a log, but didn't manage more than five to six hours until I was ready to go again. How could anyone sleep at a time like this?

Tuesday, day three of the expedition, I'd planned to be an easy, almost free day, so I could bond with Shy Boy on the ground. It turned out to be a crucial moment because on the ground I was a different entity from the 'man on horse' he'd learned to trust.

He accepted me rubbing and stroking him. I ran my hands all over him and down his legs. He followed me around. We worked with the surcingle again and made good headway. It was like a day of rest for him, but good progress all the same. He had plenty of time to eat, drink and even have a lie down in the afternoon sun. We stood around together, walked together and Shy Boy was allowing me into his life and certainly appeared to be under no pressure at all. This was a whole new world for him. We used Tuesday to deepen a relationship which I hoped would carry us into Wednesday in a manner so as to allow him to accept his first saddle, bridle and rider.

At the break of day of Wednesday, we rode about a mile and a half to the west and then down into a canyon we'd discovered. Aside from being an effective location for the first saddle and rider, this was an area of incredible beauty. Totally invisible as you looked across the high desert floor 150 feet above the bottom of this canyon, you had to ride right to the rim of it before you could view the spectacular sight below. About 300 feet wide for most of its half mile length, it had a year-round stream meandering through.

The stream was liberally punctuated with huge California sycamores. One would guess some of them to be more than two hundred years old with trunks six to eight feet in diameter. Bare of leaves at this time of year, the California sycamore stands like tortured skeletons which artists have been trying to duplicate on canvas for centuries. Their white bark and twisted limbs are unique to the world of sycamores, a specie that is in existence virtually worldwide. Rocks had been ground into sand by water's action over the millennium and the stream had spread layers of it over a flat stone-free surface for very much of the canyon floor.

That's why we chose this place, safe for Shy Boy's feet and the rider, too, should he be unfortunate enough to get bucked off. It was a choice effective for us, but might have been chosen by Frederick Remington, Charles Russell or Ansel Adams for a different purpose all together.

We rode down a trail zigzagging to the canyon floor. Caleb was on Tari. I rode George and led Shy Boy beside me. The camera crew and some of the ranch hands used four-wheel drive vehicles to ferry all the equipment into place.

Pat Russell and Scot Silvera had the riding equipment, a snaffle bit, my surcingle, a small exercise saddle, saddle pads and a stock saddle. We were ready.

The surcingle was no trouble; we'd been through that the evening before. Next I asked him to accept the small exercise saddle, and he said 'no way.' It was just too much leather to suit him. Yet, after a little coaxing, he was allowing me to put it on without any problem.

The stock saddle was looked on by Shy Boy as an insurmountable obstacle to the progress of our relationship. It was a very spooky thing, this stock saddle. It was out of the question that such an object was meant to go on his back. It took half an hour to persuade him we could be trusted. Again this is the advantage of join-up, because once the first link is forged, the rest falls into

182

place if you're reasonable. He accepted the stock saddle off and on several times and from both sides.

Next was the biggest step of all, I introduced him to Scott Silvera, who'd be the first person to ride him. Shy Boy was suspicious of the new face and reared away from Scott. We took time out for Shy Boy to become acquainted with Scott, he smelled his clothes, felt the rubbing on his neck and on the bony parts of his forehead.

Scott Silvera then slowly and carefully put a toe in the stirrup. Shy Boy jumped back and struck out with his front foot.

We all had to keep calm at this point. There should be a compete lack of urgency in any situation like this. Horses need patient handling. If you act like you've only got fifteen minutes, it'll take all day; if you act like you've got all day, it might take fifteen minutes.

After taking some more time to acquaint Scott with Shy Boy, Scott once more had his foot in the stirrup. Shy Boy was accepting him, so far… Scott lifted himself up very carefully, and swung his leg across. His rear touched the saddle, light as a feather.

This was a very emotional moment for me. The desire to see this happen, and for others to recognise it, was buried deep and it was like an explosion. The reality was a gift of great happiness and a sense of closure. I had achieved what I set out to do.

I was overwhelmed with emotion and I yelled out in triumph when Scott rode him off. Within five minutes Shy Boy was a relaxed horse.

We rode around the canyon for around half an hour to school Shy Boy and get him used to the idea of being ridden while we were on this soft terrain. He didn't put a foot wrong.

Next we intended to ride back to Pat Russell's ranch. I was on George, Caleb on his own horse and Scott on Shy Boy.

Three abreast we rode up out of that canyon, little Shy Boy performing like he'd done this all his life. We cantered up to the ranch house without a care in the world. We'd done it. I was virtually speechless with excitement.

Here I was, nearly forty-five years after my first experiments, with Dr

Miller, animal behaviourist, Carol Childerley, the Wildwatch arbitrator, along with the entire film crew, who'd been watching these events right from the start. We were greeted by a good sized group of people clapping and cheering our achievement.

Some of our closest friends had come to join-up, optimistic that the adventure would be successful; John and JoAnn Jones, Brian and Cheryl Russell, were standing beside Pat and Laurel and the rest of the happy group greeting us as we rode triumphantly to the ranch house. It was an incredible turnaround.

Needless to say, I felt wonderful and filled with pride for Shy Boy. It was perhaps the most meaningful victory to have come my way for a lot of years. We looked after our horses and then adjourned to a proper celebration with a barbecue, music and story-telling as the sun set over the Pacific, far below and to the west of us.

The crew even managed to get on film the two old cynics from the Maverick Saloon in Santa Ynez who, on seeing the successful party coming home said, 'Well, they can put a man on the moon, I guess he can bring back a mustang'.

When we got back to Flag Is Up, Shy Boy was taken to live at Ron Roll's place, in Buellton. Ron is a former student of mine who has his own training establishment just down the road from me. Shy Boy has lived there since the film was completed. Like many captured mustangs, the first thing he did in his new life was to grow taller and to put on weight. On the range life is often hard, grazing meagre, and the constant need to keep moving means mustangs tend to stay lean. When I first saw him that day in Paso Robles, Shy Boy was about 13 hands, two inches. He now stands about 14 hands, one inch and weighs about 975 pounds, about 100 pounds more than he did previously. He's ridden every day and is doing just fine. He is a joy to be around and to ride. He's doing everything that a little mustang like him enjoys doing.

Shy Boy will always hold a special place in my heart and our involvement together has been continuous. It was fate that brought us together; he just happened to be the one allocated to me at that adoption event in Paso Robles, but we're firmly linked now. We shared this bit of horse history; 'Shy Boy, The Horse That Came in From the Wild'.

SHY BOY GOES PUBLIC

I stood in front of a television camera while behind me there was a bank of around forty phones. They had shown the film of Shy Boy in America and I'd said my piece; suddenly the phones were ringing non-stop. It was phenomenal. Each phone call pledged a sum of money from an individual. They'd put out the Shy Boy film on PBS (Public Broadcasting Stations) and there were fund-raising events during which I was invited to comment on the film. The intention was that those who'd watched and who'd believed this film to be a service to mankind, were invited to pledge money to the PBS station which depended on such charitable donations for their existence.

They had a computer which measured how much money was coming in and it wasn't a trickle, it poured in. The audience was reporting the most wonderful reaction to the film. This was very satisfying as the more ears and eyes that received the message, the closer I would come to my goal of leaving the world a better place for horses and people. Each individual who felt strongly enough to ring the station and pledge their money, I counted as an ally in this initiative to improve our understanding and treatment of horses.

It was the same all over. From Washington, DC to Little Rock, Arkansas and Dallas, Texas, the local PBS stations were breaking records in raising funds on the strength of showing this programme. In Dallas they raised $59,000 in one night. The PBS station in Denver asked me to comment on the film over the phone and donations leapt from their expected $1,800 to nearly four times that much.

Possibly it's a measure of how much the USA values the mustang. The mustang is an icon of American history and to some extent we attach to the mustang the same characteristics as we'd like to see in ourselves as a nation: strong, wild at heart, occupying a great, open landscape, but above all free. Shy Boy's adventure touched a nerve and it was gratifying to me to elicit such a positive response on my home territory, the USA.

ON TOUR IN AMERICA

There's more to tell regarding Shy Boy – particularly his return to the wild. But I'd like to describe first my American tour and then move on to a particularly difficult horse called Blushing ET.

Our first demonstration was in the Riverdale Equestrian Centre in Brooklyn, New York. From there we went to Toronto, Canada and then down to Houston, Texas.

It can be understood just from this section of our itinerary that we were bouncing up and down the north American continent that autumn in order to coincide with dates available at the different venues. This was a serious amount of travelling.

Added to this was the problem that any crew we hired would have no idea what these demonstrations entailed. They'd all be first-timers. In any event, we were lucky to have a core crew whose enthusiasm overcame their being inexperienced at this 'road show' business. We had a road manager, lead rider, back-up rider, official photographer and so on. We even had young Christian Bunneman who ventured over from Germany to volunteer his assistance for the experience of the American Join-Up tour. He, as well as the others, were exceptional in their attitude and abilities.

The demonstration at the New York Riverdale Equestrian Center was our first in America in front of a paying audience; we were walking into the unknown. In England, I've become aware of how to conduct the demonstrations and the level of enthusiasm and interest they generate. Here, it might be different. I was in what was for me new territory with an audience steeped in traditional horsemanship. I just didn't have a clue how it would go down.

We demonstrated join-up on two young horses and they joined-up perfectly. The language of Equus could be seen to be working; it was predictable and measurable. The presentation went off without a mishap. The lapel microphone worked; my voice didn't dry up.

The reaction of the American audience was just the most gratifying thing.

Above: Monty's wife Pat and son Marty enjoy a standing ovation for Monty at the conclusion of one of the book launch events.

Overleaf: Sapphire Lake in Sierra Nevarda, California.

Previous page: View from Pat and Monty's home on Flag Is Up Farms, Solvang, California.

Left: Deer behind Monty and Pat's home.

193

*Above: Wild flowers in the
California desert.*

Opposite: Valley of Fire, Nevada.

*Above: Join-up on Flag Is Up with a
new two-year-old.*

*Previous page: Monty conducts a
demonstration during a corporate
conference.*

A two year-old-says, 'Just to show
you it's my first saddle…'

Above: 'Positive reward'.

*Overleaf: Full house at book launch
event in Houston.*

It was a marvellous experience. It left my son, Marty and I standing there looking at each other and saying, this demonstration of new techniques in dealing with horses is a message that is valuable to people here in the USA, just as much if not more than overseas.

We were happy, to say the least.

We couldn't have know then, as we stood shaking our heads in disbelief, that this first event at the Riverdale Equestrian Center marked the low spot of our tour and that the approval of the audience would rise steadily from there.

It was an unqualified success. Our next stop was Toronto, Canada, and we had double the numbers there when we compared to New York. We needed some encouragement for sure, as there was so much trouble getting our equipment over the border between the USA and Canada. However, once we'd made it to Toronto, it was worth it. The horses they'd found for us were warm-bloods and gave a spirited demonstration with excellent results.

Then down to Houston and a dramatic change in climate and in culture. This was Texas, the deep south, and in August it is extremely hot even at night. We were booked into a building with open sides. The mosquitoes saw this nice building with all the lights blazing, which of course meant someone was inviting them inside. There they found a feast, thousands of warm-blooded people laid on for them, indeed, quite a spread. Needless to say, it was an uncomfortable audience, but in fact very impressed.

So it was New York, Toronto, Houston, Lexington, Kentucky, Spokane, Eugene, Oregon and Los Angeles – at times our itinerary read like an airline timetable. Wherever I happened to be, I was in addition pointed in various directions to talk on the television or the radio about the book and the work I do.

It was remarkable to have so many people interested in accepting my work in the most positive light. It was truly a stirring experience to have won over many in my own country to a different, gentle way of taming horses, to be accepted as having something valuable to offer, something new which could be carried on by those who are young and energetic with their lives ahead of them.

In addition, as I've come to expect, there was every now and again an occurrence which revealed the uglier side of our human nature and the cruelty which so easily, if it's allowed to, infects our everyday domestic lives.

I was signing books on one occasion, when a little girl stood on her tip-toes to push a book at me and she told me in a very soft voice that she was interested in my work. She was thin to the point of frailty and plainly of an introverted nature.

I asked her if she had a horse herself, and then I got a smile.

I asked, 'How old are you?'

'Twelve,' was her answer, but it was almost too softly spoken to be heard.

'Did you enjoy the demonstration?' I asked.

She replied, 'Very much.'

'What did you like best about it?'

'I liked the way you don't hurt the horses.'

At this point her eyes misted over, and I realised I might have a little girl on my hands who'd suffered some form of cruelty. Her empathy with 'the horse who hadn't been hurt' spoke volumes.

I asked, 'You OK?'

Her eyes filled with tears.

I asked if she had come with someone and she said, 'Yes.' I then suggested she might want to sit through the remainder of the demonstration with my assistant and we could talk afterwards. Struggling to control her tears, she agreed she would like that.

Later on I asked her who'd brought her to the show.

'My father.'

'Is he here now?'

'That's him near the refreshment stand.'

I asked, 'Is he the problem?'

At this point, she burst into tears again. I had my arm around her and my assistant was also consoling her. I left to go and talk with the father, who at this point was standing nearby. I invited him to sit down and tell me about his horses and his life in general. I made no mention of the daughter at this stage.

I then invited him to walk with me to a more private area of the building away from the people.

We began to discuss his daughter.

He told me he was a tough taskmaster and he had three older children, all of whom he'd dealt with in a similarly stern manner. These older children were grown up now and had left home.

I asked 'Do you get along with them okay?'

'No.'

Furthermore, he said this younger daughter often neglected to clean her room and do her chores when he asked her to do so. He considered it fair to smack here when these failures occurred, although he admitted he might be, on occasion, too harsh.

After an hour of intense discussion, he confessed that at times his disciplining of the girl had been inappropriate. He didn't seem to be able to control his temper. He considered himself a failure with the older children, but concluded he needed to be even tougher on the younger one to prevent a similar failure. He was frustrated and unable to cope with the duties of parenthood.

I felt driven to relate my own experiences and my own beliefs in this area. He listened intently, and in the light of what he'd seen at the demonstration and his daughter's reaction to it, he agreed that he should reassess the situation. At this point we went over to stand with his daughter and as might be imagined, it was an intense, emotional atmosphere. The father agreed to accept family counselling which would be researched and organised by someone locally.

Since then, I've received word that things have improved in that family and I often find myself wishing them well in their effort to change entrenched patterns of behaviour, which is never easy.

The American tour was a great success. There was one incident though that struck me with particular irony. I've been all over the world doing these demonstrations – and the logistics of putting them on have sometimes been very complicated as might be imagined, especially when you're far away from home. Yet, at the demonstration which was closest to home, only a two hour drive from Flag Is Up Farms, just when arrangements should have been the easiest, it went all wrong.

Pat and I arrived to find Marty in dismay because the appropriate number of staff hadn't been booked at the venue. He'd made the usual request for around thirty-five people to handle tickets, security, the setting up of the round pen, handling of horses, the management of books and video and so on.

At Los Angeles Equestrian Center, they'd taken this request lightly and had only provided two people. This was looking like a disaster.

We had a stroke of good fortune, though. As it was the closest demonstration to home, we'd scheduled a bus to bring about twenty employees of the farm to see what the boss did on tour of the USA. They were on their way.

And were they surprised to be greeted by Marty and told there was an emergency and could they undertake various duties? Thus, it was that the Flag Is Up staff were taking tickets, minding the door, setting up the demonstration, handling the seats, putting up the podium for the books and so on. It was a lucky break for us and they've earned another invitation.

In 1998, I did close to 150 horses at our demonstrations, another twenty to thirty for charitable events plus about forty at home. This total of approximately 220 considers only the north American continent and all were before audiences.

In addition, three were approximately forty head in England with another thirty-five or so in Germany, along with ten completed before audiences in Japan.

The approximately 300 head accepted their first saddle, bridle and rider in an average of twenty-seven minutes. It seems to me likely that this is a new record of sorts.

My organisation is proud of the fact that during this 1998 season we have raised $655,000 for causes which will improve the lives of horses and horse people.

BLUSHING ET

Sleeping Giant, a company from Toronto, decided in mid-1997 that they would produce a documentary involving an extremely troubled horse. This horse was to be chosen from a list of thoroughbred horses for its paranoia with the starting gate. It was their goal to film the retraining of this horse to accept the gate and racing. Research indicated that the best chance they had for a meaningful and successful project was to engage my services in this effort.

We had an extensive search to locate an appropriate subject, contacting individuals such as trainers, starting gate crewmen, jockeys and people familiar with and in a position to see this type of horse on a daily basis.

Sean McCarthy is a former employee of Flag Is Up Farms as well as the student who has spent the most time working with me in an effort to rehabilitate horses with this problem. Sean happened to be with me in England when I was called to Henry Cecil's yard in Newmarket to deal with North Country, an incredibly troubled individual, who eventually came right and won races.

Responses began to fly in from all directions, demonstrating the depth and severity of this problem in racing. It was Sean, though, who came up with the strongest prospect to fill the bill. He indicated that the horse was recently placed in training with Janine Sahadi in Santa Anita. He told me that Ms Sahadi had been warned that Blushing ET had a problem with the starting gate, but little did she know what she really had on her hands. The first trip to the gate resulted in a broken hand for his handler, Zane Baze, and a loose horse on the race-course.

As Sean investigated, he was to discover that Blushing ET, a two-year old by Blushing John, was sent to California from Florida. The stories of his troubles there would curl your hair. One confidential report was that there were many sessions of aggressive beatings which ended with Blushing ET lying flat on the ground and refusing to get up for ten to fifteen minutes at a time. This fellow said that the horse became extremely aggressive and had injured handlers in the process to force him to enter the starting gate. He went on to say that Blushing ET even learned to be aggressive while lying on the ground twenty to thirty yards from the gate. The conclusion of everyone contacted was Blushing ET was a hopeless case and it was not humanely possible to cause him to overcome his phobia.

I accepted Blushing ET as my challenge and I must admit that I went into this project with a degree of confidence that woefully underestimated the determination of this horse never to allow the starting gate back into his life. For those who read my first book, you will quickly realise that I had a lot of experience with bad horses at the starting gate. There were dozens, but most prominently were Lomitas, North Country, and the horse that I have for seven years regarded as my greatest challenge in this category, Prince of Darkness.

Aptly named, Prince of Darkness was, as I have often said, a great teacher when it came to dealing with horses with starting gate problems. I still hold that to be true, but if that is the case, then Blushing ET is an entire university. I remember being deeply embarrassed when Prince of Darkness took me eight days to bring to a point which would allow him to race. Little did I know that I was about to embark upon a challenge which would take me eighty days.

Blushing ET knew things about defending himself against human beings of ill intent that Prince of Darkness had never heard of. Humility is a wonderful virtue when it comes to working with horses with problems and Blushing ET was very quick to remind me that I had allowed my humility to slip below the optimum level. Looking back over all of it now, I realise that one of my problems was to fail to fully observe the reasons why both Prince of Darkness and Blushing ET felt the need to resist the starting gate.

Prince of Darkness was in training with Sir Mark Prescott in Newmarket, England. Sir Mark is a good horseman with a compassionate attitude towards the flight animal and a mind quick to know when he's gone far enough. Prince of Darkness had an extreme problem with the starting gate and a minimal problem with human beings. Blushing ET had a violent phobia against the starting gate and a deep seated hatred for human beings. I believe that this hatred was justified and born out of abject brutality toward him. I should have been more sensitive to these differences which would have prepared me better to cope with the eighty days and lessen the surprise of it all.

Blushing ET was transported from Santa Anita to Flag Is Up Farms in November 1997, and I began my work without the slightest doubt that I would be prepared to send him back to Ms Sahadi with time to spare for an opening date at Santa Anita on December 26.

By the end of the first day's session, I realised that I was dealing with a new dimension in troubled horses. Blushing ET began very early to dive at me with teeth bared, only because I was trying to put a protective blanket on him. The first two or three days would be used up in simply securing the blanket and getting him close enough to the starting gate to enter an enclosed area I had constructed on each side of the gate itself. Going into the gate by moving forward was a total impossibility through the first five or six sessions.

I was able however, to back him in a manoeuvre I have come to respect with virtually every horse at the gate. I have learned that the horse that won't back well on the lead, will nearly always fail to move forward well on the lead.

In an effort to keep his aerobic fitness intact, we gave him a good canter each day as well as a ride around the farm from time to time in an attempt to freshen his mind and encourage him to see human beings in a better light.

Felipe Castro worked with him every day, but the problem at the gate showed little overall improvement. He gave me the feeling that there just might be a piece of the puzzle missing. Blushing ET taught all of us so much about the effect of trauma. I found I could go only so far with him and then it felt as if I hit a brick wall and I couldn't put my finger on the cause of it.

He was kind and peaceful in the stable, the lads could groom him, bandage him and generally manage all his stable requirements. Even washing him and running water down his legs did not bother him, but put anything foreign around his hocks and he would explode ears back and thrashing. I had the strongest suspicion that all of this had to do with the jockey's foot rails which travel along each side of the individual starting stalls and meet the horse squarely at the flank and the stifle, an extremely sensitive area.

The crisis point of this horse's remedial treatment came the day after Christmas. The day before I had made an important decision while watching Blushing ET's extreme concern with the side rails. He was so beset by those rails touching him in the flanks that it seemed I was never going to get anywhere until we could get him confident that they wouldn't harm him. I simply couldn't believe that the use of the blanket plus the hours of work had not taken effect more dramatically and allowed him to accept it.

One realisation that came to me was that in earlier attempts I was unable to put this horse on the long lines. If you dropped the line over his hip and along his side, he would absolutely go berserk. He would kick out with his back feet and strike the ground with the front, as though he was extremely angry and was going to do anything he could to get away from the lines. He was fierce to the extent that he was without doubt going to hurt himself, or me, if it continued. In addition to kicking out and striking the ground, there was an intermittent aggressive attitude which was, 'I'm going to come and get you'. He would march around you, a line on each side and then attack with such force, I was unable to pull him off me. I believed he could have killed me anytime he chose. I must confess, at those moments, I had absolutely no control.

It was late evening and I was watching a football game on television when I realised I barely knew who was playing. My mind was totally transfixed on Blushing ET. I decided to go down to the barn and tackle this problem. I drove to the round pen, after mustering some assistance. When I got there it was already dark. I put the lights on. Caroline Baldock and Faith Grey were both with me and it seemed a very lonely spot to be even with the ladies there; it was frightening.

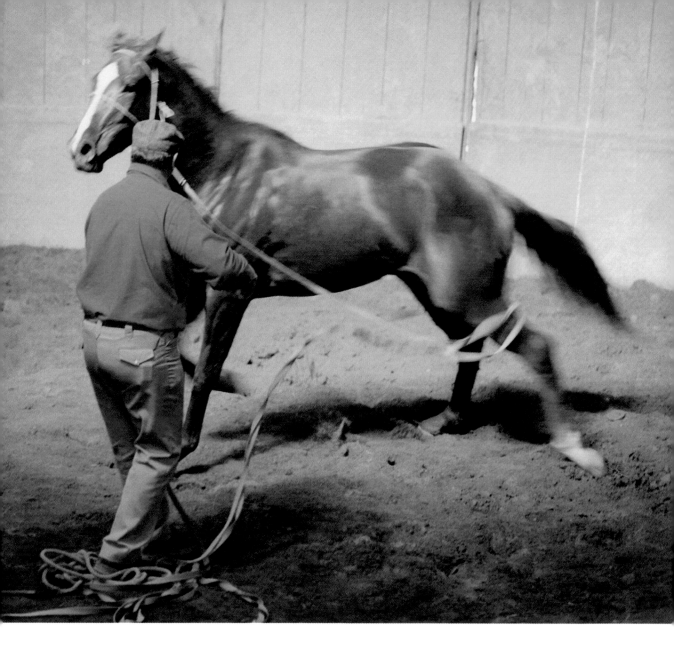

Above: Blushing ET saying,
'Anything that touches my hocks
will get kicked away.'

Overleaf: Blushing ET
and Monty spending
quality time together.

214   *Above: Join-up with Blushing ET.*

Above: Blushing ET works hard to help me invent the new system for training at the starting stalls. Felipe Castro is riding.

Above left and right: 12 July, 1998,
Blushing ET wins his first race at
Hollywood Park.

Previous page: Jockey Alex Solis on
Blushing ET, on the way to victory.

Overleaf: Hector Valadez and
Monty work at the starting
stalls with a 'student'.

*Above: Monty and Dually in a rare
moment during these busy days.*

*Opposite: A morning walk in the mist
on Flag Is Up.*

When we arrived at the stables, I went in and saddled Dually. I checked the reins back to the saddle horn and left him standing in his stall. To this day, I don't really know exactly why I did that, but there was something in my mind, subconsciously perhaps, that I might need Dually to help me in this scenario. I never tacked Dually before in this sort of situation. There was something else going on in my mind.

I took Blushing ET from the stable to the round pen and went inside, deciding to leave his stable blanket on him. This was to lessen the effect of a foreign feeling of the line near his hip and stifle. I felt confident that with the blanket in place I could encourage him to accept the line and after some work, he would agree to accept it without the blanket. Once more I was guilty of giving his phobias far too little respect.

I went into the pen with complete confidence that I would spend an hour or two that evening and get him to accept the lines without any trouble. When the line was first placed over his hip I was amazed once more how wrong I could be. He was just as violent as he had been without the stable blanket. I was certain it would cushion the lines sufficiently so that he would not go into his violent mode … not so. I did everything I new to get him to settle and accept the lines … no luck.

I was in deep trouble. As the minutes went by it was clear to see he only became more angry, making intermittent darts toward me with ears back and teeth bared despite my calm and deliberate attempts. One can hardly have a feeling so dramatically fearsome as a large grown horse coming at you in a full-on frontal attack. I tried to double him around, pulling the off line so as to get his head away from me. It just didn't work. He was too strong.

Caroline and Faith jumped down from the viewing stand and opened the gate so I could escape to safety. I walked around on the outside wondering what in the world I had done to have this happen. The more I thought about it, the more I realised that there was this incredible fear in him of anything

Opposite: Monty and Dually fade into the mist between
a line of poplar trees on Flag Is Up.

along his sides. He had experienced the side rails to the extent that anything touching his sides in the area of the flank and stifle would evoke instant terror. The abuse he had received at the hand of humans while attempting to cope with the natural aversion compounded his negative experience. The harder they whipped him, the more he blamed the rails and later, the human as well.

I walked up to the ramp to the viewing deck where I could see him dragging the long lines around the pen behind him. I had to leave them on because I was fleeing for my life. It dawned on me that possibly with the use of strips of cloth tied to the stirrups, I could get him used to objects along his sides and near his hocks. These cloth strips would tear away under pressure unlike the driving lines which would not because of their strength.

I went into the stable and got some girth covers and saddle towels. I then returned to the round pen where I saw that he had relaxed enough to allow me to tie the cloths to the stirrups. He kicked them and fought them very hard for a while and then he finally began to settle a bit. It seemed that he was going to become accustomed to them. I gradually lengthened the strips so that they came back around his legs.

Again he kicked at them but eventually I felt I could try the long lines again with the stable blanket still in place. The noise was incredible when his feet hit the side of the pen. You wouldn't have wanted to be between them and the wall. I hadn't achieved much. I got the same reaction and this time he almost nailed me. He charged and nearly got me in his teeth as once more I slipped out the gate with a front foot less than an inch from making contact.

I paced up and down outside racking my brain; what can I do? All of a sudden the light came on. What if I mounted Dually and rode him into the round pen? Would Blushing ET accept Dually? I would be up off the ground and in less danger. Consequently, I rode Dually into the round pen and gathered up the long lines. I put one over Blushing ET's back and the other directly to the bit and began to drive him without putting the lines over his hips.

As I did, I could see that this was rather acceptable. It seemed he was coming around allowing me to handle him from the back of Dually. I could actually put my reins over the saddle horn and guide Dually with just my legs and voice. After a few minutes it seemed it was going well enough. Again I put the line over his hips to be in the regular driving line pattern. As soon as the line went over the hip, be began the same outrageous behaviour. He kicked, biting and striking out, and twice made fairly strong attacks on Dually. I was able to jump Dually forward and avert Blushing ET's charge, throwing my arms up to get him to stop.

I began to see I had slightly the upper hand while in the saddle or, at least, a neutral position rather than a wholly vulnerable one. I took the line off the nearside and left the line on the offside. I began to ride in a big circle so that as I crossed behind ET, I could bring the line near his hock. When it touched his hock, he would kick fiercely. I would allow this kicking until there was the slightest pause and then immediately I would take the line off his hock, riding in a circle around the front of him so as to bring the line close to the other hock. I would repeat the process on the opposite side vigilant to quickly reward any improvement by once more riding away. Soon I was able to get a pattern where I could hold it against his hock and see that the kicking was dramatically subsiding. I would then ride in a big circle sometimes at a trot and let it come against the other hock repeating the same process.

It was amazing to watch him learn to communicate with me. I could see the enlightenment come over him. When he stopped kicking, I would take the line off his hock. After a period of time, I could ride so as to let it touch his hock and he wouldn't kick and I'd ride way. The instant that happened, I was on a course to succeed. I guess this comes under the heading, 'that if all learning is zero to ten, then the most important part of learning is zero to one.'

I think it is appropriate to note that this exercise strongly suggests a relationship between horses and children. I think this lesson dramatically demonstrates that the crying child is rewarded when the parent picks it up while it is still crying. Checking to see that the child is physically okay is certainly advisable and appropriate. Once the parent is satisfied, however, allowing crying to continue until there is a short break, and then rewarding quickly by holding close and caressing generously, can be extremely effective. Then the child will be receiving positive reward upon ceasing crying instead of the other way around.

After about a half hour of this work, I was able to put both lines on, run them through the stirrups of the saddle that was placed over the blanket and drive him around the pen. The more steps I took the better he got. Every once in a while, he would lightly revert and I would go back to square one. These periods of regression rapidly became shorter, however, and it seemed I was making great progress.

Before the evening was over, I was able to drive him around the pen without any problem. There was an intermittent bout with failure when I decided he was going well enough that I could step off Dually and drive Blushing ET from the ground. This was a mistake and immediately he went back to the aggressive mode again. That was the moment I realised the depth of this horse's hatred for men on the ground. After this night I noticed that anytime a man would come near him when loading in the starting stalls, he would worry. If anyone walks behind him, you can see him get ready to fight. I suppose he is still that way to a degree and I doubt he will ever forget what they did to him. But that night, between six until nine thirty, was a 'course change' for ET and me. After that, I could drive him on the long lines through the starting stalls.

It was the beginning of success with Blushing ET. I could drive him walking in circles, right through the starting gate and eventually without a surge of panic. From that point on it was a matter of using his own language, going step by step through each of the procedures and he began to behave more like a normal horse.

He stands alone as the most difficult horse I have ever dealt with in this area. One interesting part to all this is that you learn when you are challenged and, if you are worth your salt in your discipline, you will rise to the task. You will use your brain and eliminating any violence as an option, you will work out ways to communicate your desires, respecting your student's rights.

In 1992, I was certain that Prince of Darkness was the ultimate challenge. That was well short of the mark. In 1998, I am fairly certain that Blushing ET is the ultimate challenge. I hope I never see a horse that is more difficult.

Blushing ET provided me with the information that I needed to construct a new facility. I believe that this invention, should horsemen take advantage of it, will cause any horse, no matter how badly damaged they are at the starting gate, to accept it. My design is what I call the 'hallway' and is a circular set of panels that allows a horse to leave the starting gate and return to it through the use of this special device. If the industry comes to understand it, it will become a feature of race-tracks all over the world. It will allow young horses to get their first experience at the starting gate without the stress they often encounter. I have spoken with several tracks in the US which are interested in being the very first to test this procedure. I am excited about it. I think that my work with Blushing ET will be the catalyst in a formula to help horses worldwide with the starting gate.

A sad part to this story is that there are still horses everywhere who are trying to tell human beings that they are being treated unfairly and that humans just don't seem to understand them. This only serves to prove how incompetent I've been when for so many years I failed to understand why all those horses saw fit to fight the starting stalls. The only solace I have is that nobody else did either. Prince of Darkness was a teacher; Blushing ET was a university. The lessons of Blushing ET if heeded, will certainly help to make the world a better place for horses. If trainers and people who make decisions about horses in racing will listen to the lessons of Blushing ET, then horses will have an easier time at the starting stalls.

The results of my work with Blushing ET could hardly be more gratifying. He won two races consecutively, one a maiden race at Hollywood Park on July 12 1998, and another, an allowance race in Del Mar on the turf with a purse of $55.200 on August 26 1998. Blushing ET is healthy and sound and perhaps has more victories in store for his owners.

Knowledgeable people through the American racing industry are calling this nothing short of a miracle. Once more I am compelled to express gratitude to the specie Equus for being so tolerant, patient and understanding of the shortcomings of the human race. Blushing ET is a perfect example of each of those qualities. I thank this particular individual for being such an effective teacher through the countless hours that he waited for me to learn.

SHY BOY'S RETURN TO THE WILD

This book has been inspired by Shy Boy. It was an adventure which I never thought I'd have the opportunity to undertake and which to my amazement and gratification unfolded with hardly a hitch, although not without anxiety and challenges along the way. On the whole, it went better than I thought possible. The airing of the BBC documentary on Shy Boy has made the little mustang something of a celebrity. People have come to our farm from all over the continent and many parts of Europe just to see this horse.

The programme also threw up a million conversations, questions and enquiries. Literally hundreds of people have asked me this one question, 'Do you think Shy Boy is better off now or would he rather be wild?'

It was a question I had to answer.

Obviously, I don't know. I can't read his thoughts. I can observe a steady, contented horse who is happy in his work and affectionate in his dealings with those people responsible for his care. But I can't judge whether or not he is longing after the open range.

However, it seemed to me that there was one way to tell if a horse enjoyed doing something and that is, give him the opportunity of doing it. This sort of logic reminds me of a saying I'd offer to my students, 'You say your horse loves to jump; well, put him in a field full of jumps and if he chooses to run around and jump them all by himself, I'll believe you'. It's not such an out of the way idea, some horses have been known to do just that.

In the case of Shy Boy, there was a large number of people wanting to know, if he were given the chance, which would he chose, the life of a domesticated animal, or that of a true mustang?

This, yes, we could answer. We could take him back to the wild.

The Twissleman family was due to round-up 350 head of cattle around the first of March 1998, almost a year after Shy Boy was cut out of the feral herd there in the high California desert.

I suggested that Caleb Twissleman ride Shy Boy on that round-up, and that at an opportune moment, we would leave him in the company of the exact same herd which he was taken from. We would give him the choice: he could stay with the wild ones or come back to us.

I had a film crew, four-wheel drive trucks, and aircraft and all of the necessities for documenting whatever the heck we might see. Dr Robert Miller agreed to be with us start to finish to observe and comment on the psychological aspects of the study. Most of all, however, he took charge of the safety and treatment of all animals involved.

All agreed that this would be a valid postscript to the Shy Boy story. We went into the planning stage. There would be designated areas to cover, dividing their ranch into three separate sections. I decided to ride The Cadet for the high country part of the round-up. Caleb and I chose the western part of the property because that was the area where the herd of horses was most often spotted.

On Monday morning, 12 March 1998 we loaded our horses on the trailer. Shy Boy, The Cadet, Big Red Fox, Arnie and Dually were fit and ready to go. Pat and I had invited Caroline Baldock to come along and assist by making suggestions as to how we function according to the outline that we had drawn up for the project.

We headed north on High 101 through the coastal towns of central California, turning east at Santa Margarita. We proceeded through some of the most beautiful mountains our state has to offer progressing toward the high desert we had been to eleven months earlier. Winter rains had turned the country a deep Irish green and the wild flowers were just beginning to unfurl across the south-facing slopes.

We were more than 3,000 feet above sea level before we levelled off on that portion of the high desert called the Carissa Plains. They were bedecked by a green carpet, winter grass less than an inch in height, barely a tree in sight. Soda Lake, however, was visible thirty miles away, silvery, flat as a sheet of glass cut exactly to fit the indentation of the land.

The San Andreas Fault runs right through the middle of this vast expanse. We in fact, were to, camp right over it on the north margin of the plain.

We had cell phones so that everybody could co-ordinate exactly how to get to the campsite. As Pat and I stood there as the crew began to arrange the trucks and trailers, I was suddenly struck by the beauty of this place: the scent of sage and clover carried on the breeze, the huge mountains framing the vast plain, the sky overhead and the palpable silence of it all. It was incredible.

I saddled my horses and began my ritual procedures preparing them for the project which would begin the following day. I allowed each of them to run free for short periods of time which is a normal course of action for me. As I rode back toward the camp, I became aware that they had a fire going as the smell of burning oak wood permeated the air.

A high pitched wail cut the silence. Then a chorus of howls answered. It was as if a thousand dogs were answering the question. It was a pack of coyotes, which couldn't have been more than a quarter of a mile away. It was frightening to those in the group who were not familiar with coyotes because the sound curdles your blood; but to those of us who knew how harmless they really are, it was just a reminder that we were back in the wilderness. It was cold, so similar to that time eleven months earlier when it seemed I would freeze before touching Shy Boy.

At sun up, Rowly, Cathy and Caleb Twissleman came driving into the camp from the main headquarters. They had two huge trailers, one for horses and one for equipment. We prepared for the day in very short order and Rowly co-ordinated the splitting of us into various teams. The job at hand was to gather cattle and it was time to go. The question we'd be asking Shy Boy would follow the round-up itself.

As the sun came up and began to warm us a bit, I was once more struck by how gorgeous it was up there. With Caleb on Shy Boy and myself on The Cadet, we headed for the north-east corner of this vast acreage. Caleb knew every nook and corner. After all, he was born and raised there. We went up through a canyon and over a ridge and found ourselves moving along the face of a steep mountainside through sparse chemise brush and sage. A jackrabbit jumped out and nearly stopped my heart. The Cadet took flight and I had to fight to regain my seat in the saddle. Caleb, off to my right, laughed at the sight. Shy Boy hardly took any notice at all. He had seen plenty of jackrabbits in his time.

Soon after reaching the top of the ranch, we began to put together a sizeable number of cattle, which is what we were there for, after all. We started working them downwards near the east margin of the property. We had about sixty head by then, but I could see many more out in front of us.

We were probably 2,000 feet higher than the corrals at this point, and through the binoculars I could see the other teams driving cattle toward them. It seemed everything was running smoothly.

Caleb and I pressed on picking up more cattle along the way. At one point we dipped into a canyon with a significant flow of water at the bottom of it, but an awful smell, as we descended, worsened steadily. It was the odour of rotten eggs. I asked Caleb if he knew what it was and he replied that it was a sulphur spring. It was time for the horses to drink, but The Cadet wouldn't go near the water. Shy Boy however was happy to take a drink of it and Caleb allowed him a few mouthfuls. Shy Boy was educated in ways of nature and eleven months of domestication hadn't taken from him the knowledge that this water wouldn't hurt him and in nature, it might be a long time before he saw water again.

As we were beginning our descent to the holding corrals, I noticed about ten head off to one side of our herd. I suggested to Caleb that he go on with the main troop while I galloped off to gather these extras. As I approached the cattle, I noticed Shy Boy's horses in the brush beyond them. I turned the cows towards Caleb's main group and did nothing to disturb the horses.

We drove the cattle down to the holding corrals where 200 head or so were waiting for us.

From a vantage point a couple of hundred feet above the pens, the beauty was stunning. Stretching out in front of us was about thirty miles of the Carissa Plains. The colours of the cattle, the horses and the people painted a backdrop that was frankly awesome. The floor of the desert was awash with wild flowers and, while I can't see in colour, I can certainly perceive the variations. There were almost 400 cattle strung out below us as though the landscape was wearing a necklace of variegated colours, the red and white of the Herefords, the Angus, jet black, and the Brahmans, grey, blue and buckskin.

There was Shy Boy, cantering to the flank of the herd, jumping ditches in dodging the sage. It was better than any oil painting could be. We guided our cattle into the holding corrals, and I was pleased to see that Shy Boy was a valuable member of the team. He actually appeared to be quite proud of himself.

Once we had the cattle corralled, it was time to have some lunch and I must say it was a festive atmosphere around the picnic tables. The crew had Garth Brooks blasting out loud from the cab of one of the vehicles. The saddles were removed, the horses fed and watered and their legs hosed down. An hour or two of rest was certainly welcome by all, animal and human.

One of the ranch hands had reported that the herd had begun to graze closer to the camp, probably intrigued by our horses and the sound of Garth Brooks. This might play into our hands.

With lunch and a good rest behind us, it was time to cut out the designated yearlings from the herd. I was on Dually. He was doing what he loved to do best. Dually was a cutting horse of world class proportion, but here we were working, rather than competing. There's nothing quite like it, done for real.

Caleb had remounted Shy Boy and together they were watching Dually, the old pro, cutting out the young cattle. Caleb called out that he'd like to give Shy Boy a try and I agreed. He must have been watching Dually closely as he seemed to be getting the hang of it in very short order. Shy Boy earned a round of applause from our group for preventing a steer from getting back to the herd.

By the time we had finished cutting out the yearlings, it was four in the afternoon and the shadows were getting long. A camp fire was lit and the horses were settled down with a good flake of hay. The cattle who were not chosen to go to the headquarters were released. The sunset painted colours on the underside of the clouds and the air was filled with sounds of the cows calling and calves replying. With over 300 tramping through the sage, the air was filled with an aromatic mixture that wafted over us teasing the olfactory sense in a fashion rarely experienced by normal human beings who live in civilised areas.

It was nearly five o'clock when Caleb and I sat down by the fire to discuss the business at hand, the release of Shy Boy. The ranch hands had reported that the free-ranging ranch horses were just out of sight on the ridge to the north of the camp. They took a couple of their saddle horses toward the south-east of us to tempt the feral herd to investigate. It worked perfectly and the herd appeared atop the right in sight of the camp. There were about twenty of them silhouetted as the sun set, edging them in gold.

Shy Boy was the only horse in camp that noticed them. His ears were locked in their direction. He was transfixed, his big black eyes focused on the herd. I said to Caleb, 'This is what we came for; it's time to see what happens.' Caleb's face wore a mixture of apprehension and sadness. After all, we might never see this little horse again. 'Give him a rub,' I said and took his halter off.

Immediately, Shy Boy whirled and in one graceful jump he was in a full gallop headed straight for the herd on the horizon. Fear shot through me. Shy Boy's movement, attitude and direction was with absolute certainty, strongly suggesting he was going back to the wild for good.

It was nearly dark, yet we could see him clearly when he joined with the group of horses on the ridge. I thought it probable that the herd would reject him; after all, for eleven months he'd been on a different feed and water. He'd lived almost a hundred miles away from them, surely they had forgotten him. I was amazed to see just the opposite; they accepted him without a murmur, as if he had never been away from them. There were no challenges, no biting or kicking. The last thing we saw before darkness was Shy Boy out front, leading the herd over the ridge.

We were all amazed at the level of acceptance expressed by the herd. I had to work hard to convince Caleb that it wasn't over yet. Shy Boy had had nothing but kind treatment. He'd had a warm bed, good food and fresh water every day of the eleven months we had him. I felt he'd had a wonderful time with us, but I wasn't sure of myself.

I didn't sleep all night. I walked around making excuses for things I had to do, but found myself doing little but watching the sky lines around the camp looking for a familiar silhouette.

At five a.m. I wandered through the horses and the cattle in the pen. I continued to watch, but there was nothing. By six a.m. we could see the hill-side clearly enough to know that Shy Boy was nowhere near us. Was he gone forever? Had he chosen the wild?

Rowly Twissleman called out that we should stoke up the fire and get the breakfast going. We had to drive the yearlings back to the headquarters. Caleb was dragging his feet, which was uncharacteristic for him.

We all ate breakfast as slowly as possible hoping to delay long enough for Shy Boy to make an appearance. Caleb, of course, had lost his mount so he was looking begrudgingly to having to ride home in a truck.

I saddled The Cadet and decided to brush out his tail. Strange the things you will do when trying to kill time. Then I heard Caleb's little sister, Tara, call out, 'Hey, look there; it's Shy Boy. He's come back.'

I looked up sharply and I could see movement in the sage brush. There was a single horse, about 300 yards to the north, on a hill just rising about us. He was moving in our direction. The rising sun cast a bright light across the ridge, as if it was lit by a spotlight. The horse was now approaching a clearing in the sage brush. He trotted right to the centre of the clearing and stopped as if it was a theatrical stage. He stood square in the middle of this clearing and looked beautiful.

It was Shy Boy.

Everybody in the camp was stunned silent. It was as if time was frozen for this moment. Shy Boy remained motionless. It crossed my mind that even if he whirled and took off again, at least he had come back to say good-bye.

Shy Boy, with a very deliberate movement, turned his head to look back in the direction of the free herd. He held that position for a couple of seconds, then looked back toward the camp. He lowered his head and began to walk.

The direction he took was oblique to us. Was he still making up his mind? He moved slowly, deliberately, as if considering which way to turn. As

237

he reached the edge of the clearing, his head lifted and he broke into a trot coming squarely in our direction now. He was in the sage moving in a serpentine fashion to find his way through the brush.

About 250 yards from the camp, he broke into a full gallop. There seemed to be a path through the sage and he followed it in a zigzag fashion. In my mind I was repeating over and over, 'Come on, Shy Boy, come on home.' Caleb was standing directly behind me now.

Shy Boy was running at a full gallop straight toward us. He gave a loud, clear whinny.

He was charging straight at us, but we didn't move a muscle. I was wearing a great big smile and standing quite happily right in his path. He galloped full out and only at the last second applied the brakes and came to a stop a few yards in front of me so that I could step forward and welcome him in.

All by himself, Shy Boy exhibited his true freedom and chose to come home.

FOR FURTHER INFORMATION

My goal is to leave the world a better place, for horses and people, than I found it.

In that effort I invite you to call for further information regarding clinics, conferences, educational videos and other products at:

phone: US code + 805 688 4264
on-line: www.montyroberts.com
  and: montyroberts.co.uk
e-mail: admin@montyroberts.com

Thank you,
Monty Roberts

Below: A portrait of Monty and Dually.